INSIDER'S G
TO APPLYI
TO UNIVERSI

LRC
034
Dewsbury: (01924) 465916 ext 2286
library@kirkleescollege.ac.uk

D0345910

113046

INSIDER'S GUIDE TO APPLYING TO UNIVERSITY

KARLA FITZHUGH

2ND EDITION

Insider's Guide to Applying to University

This 2nd edition published in 2011 by Trotman, an imprint of Crimson Publishing, Westminster House, Kew Road, Richmond TW9 2ND.

First edition published in 2008.

© Trotman Publishing 2011

Author: Karla Fitzhugh

The author has asserted her moral right to be identified as the author of this book.

British Library Cataloguing in Publication Data
A catalogue record for this book is available from the British Library

ISBN: 978-1-84455-397-6

All rights reserved. No part of this publication may be reproduced, stored in a retrieval system or transmitted in any form or by any means, electronic and mechanical, photocopying, recording or otherwise without prior permission of Trotman Publishing.

Typeset by: IDSUK (Data Connection) Ltd
Printed by: L.E.G.O. SpA, Trento

INSIDER'S GUIDE TO APPLYING TO UNIVERSITY

Contents

ABOUT THE AUTHOR

 arla Fitzhugh is an author and journalist who has written extensively on higher education choice. Karla is the author of *The Virgin University Survival Guide* and has written for a number of education publications for young people, including UCAS's *YouCan* magazine, as well as a wide variety of newspapers, including the *Guardian* and *Independent*.

ACKNOWLEDGEMENTS

uch love and thanks go to Doug for his help and support during the writing of this second edition of the book.

I'm also grateful to the staff at Trotman and all the interviewees who've contributed so much to the *Insider's Guide*.

INTRODUCTION

T he writing of this second edition of the *Insider's Guide to Applying to University* coincides with record-high numbers of people applying to get into higher education, a challenging employment market for graduates and uncertainty over fees and funding.

Going to university has always offered the opportunity to study interesting subjects at a higher level and enjoy the experience of university life, and it has become even more popular for a variety of reasons. It's been heavily promoted as an ideal for young people by successive governments, and in tough economic times many courses appear to offer ways in to secure, and sometimes lucrative, careers. Mature students recently applied in record numbers too, most hoping to better their personal prospects after time spent in the workforce.

In the meantime, universities have been banned from taking on more students than their allocated quotas, and cuts are being felt throughout the higher education system, so demand has outstripped supply. This year around 700,000 applicants competed for fewer than 500,000 full-time undergraduate places.

If you're thinking about applying to university or college this year or next, there's never been a better time to equip yourself with insider advice and tips. Start early, research and prepare well, and you'll be able to give yourself the best possible chance in this competitive arena.

CHAPTER ONE
CHOOSING YOUR COURSE

 t's wise to invest plenty of effort and allow time for careful consideration at the start of the application process. Not only will it help you pick the right course, it can also dramatically increase your chances of making a successful application. Even if you already have a clear idea of the course you'd like to take, or the career path you'd like to follow, plenty of research and reflection is needed to give your communications with universities and colleges the edge.

The financial burden of gaining a higher education qualification has increased greatly in the last few years, and it may continue to rise dramatically. Consequently, the cost and quality of a degree and the employment prospects for its graduates have gained far greater importance on the list of prospective students' priorities. While funding and debt are both undoubtedly a large part of the equation for a great number of people, it's also good to enjoy what, and hopefully where, you're studying as well. Being generally happy with your choice can improve your chances of gaining higher grades, and it also reduces your chances of dropping out.

There are many lists and tables available that claim to tell you what the 'best' courses and universities are. These may be useful sometimes as part of gaining a broader overview, but should be taken with a pinch of salt on their own as the figures can be out of date or weighted according to criteria that aren't important to everyone. The 'best' course for you is the one that you're most interested in, for your own personal reasons, and the only person who can decide that is you – preferably with plenty of accurate information in front of you.

In a nutshell, successful undergraduates are committed and genuinely interested in their subject. Openness to new ideas, trying out new things and

socialising are also good. This doesn't mean you should join every society going; knowing yourself is really important. Be prepared to manage your own time and undertake a large proportion of self-directed study. **⁊**

FRASER SHADWELL, CONNEXIONS PERSONAL ADVISER

WHY GO INTO HIGHER EDUCATION?

In the past, the main motivations for going to university or college have been twofold: both to gain qualifications and to enjoy the entire university experience. Increasingly, applicants have come to look two steps ahead – focusing upon employment levels for graduates, job security, earning potential and career trajectories. It is being seen more in terms of a financial investment, as well as an investment of time and effort. More and more candidates are looking for value for money.

Higher education is a big commitment and can be hard work at times, taking you out of your comfort zone, but this can be rewarding in a variety of ways. Financial prospects for graduates tend to be better than prospects for non-graduates: people with degrees tend to earn more over their working lives and are significantly less likely to be unemployed for any length of time. Certain careers also demand specific degrees or postgraduate qualifications before you can work in them.

But it's important to look at more than the money issues when searching for a course. Studying for a degree or diploma is an opportunity to explore an interesting subject in depth, to make the most of your natural talents and to challenge yourself intellectually. It allows you to push yourself and develop new skills, expand your horizons, increase your self-confidence, meet diverse and interesting people and expand your social life.

COURSE CHOICE OVERVIEW

If you're certain that you want to go into higher education, the biggest decisions will be what to study, where to study it, how to fund yourself, and what you'd like to do after you graduate. This process can be quite complicated and time consuming, and sometimes it's difficult to know where to begin. It's easiest to break it down into smaller parts so you don't feel overwhelmed. Start by making a rough timetable for tackling each task, and create a progress file so you know where you are. You'll also be able to refer back to the file for reminders and pointers if you have moments where you get a bit lost or stuck.

Try breaking your tasks up using the headings below:

1 Think hard about your interests, talents and values.

2 Look at broad subject areas that might suit you.

3 Consider future career options.

4 Narrow subject choices down into courses.

5 Research course requirements, content, format, finance and prospects.

6 Check course standards, quality and ratings.

7 Undertake extra activities to support your application.

8 Match suitable courses with suitable environments.

9 Start to apply for your chosen courses.

10 Make applications for funding.

A recent survey suggests that up to a third of degree students say they chose the wrong course, and picking a course or institution you find you don't like increases your chances of dropping out. This can be demoralising and very costly. Putting in some time and research allows you to be more confident in your decisions, and to enjoy your course and surroundings. The more interested and happy you are, the more motivated you will be in your studies, which can gain you a better class of degree. In turn, this may open a lot of doors to you in a competitive graduate job market. Careful preparation pays off in the long run.

....

❝ I've applied to do business and marketing because I wanted a degree that would leave me with a lot of career options at the end of it. And I chose marketing as a strand of business as I am quite creative, and this is the part I have enjoyed studying most at A level. You can also take a sandwich year with these courses, which I really want to do as I think that would give me great experience and really help me to get a job after graduation. **〞**

PETE MANN, AGE 17

WHERE DO YOUR INTERESTS LIE?

At this early stage, there's no need to worry if you aren't sure about what you'd most like to study. Even if you do have quite a firm idea of subjects you're keen on, or have a specific career in mind, some of the following pointers can help you to double check that you're going in the right direction.

The right subject for you takes into account these factors:

- your personality
- your preferences
- your values
- your talents and skills
- your career aspirations.

....

❝ [A careers adviser] will be able to talk through your options with you and show you key resources. However, to get going straight away, try "idea generators" such as the Stamford test on the UCAS website or the Higher Ideas demo (www.careersoft.co.uk/Products/ Higher_Ideas). Both are free and fairly easy to use. **〞**

NIKKI BRUNNING, CONNEXIONS PERSONAL ADVISER

It isn't always easy being self-reflective but there are some exercises you can try to make it easier. For example, you could list your strengths and your weaknesses. Another interesting list to make is one of your interests versus dislikes. Gain extra perspective by asking several people who know you well where they think your strengths, weaknesses and talents lie. Yes, it can be an uncomfortable experience, and you might not always agree with everything they say, but they might come up with some striking observations that you hadn't expected, or good points you'd forgotten or were too modest to mention.

Ask a range of people for their opinions, such as:

- teachers, tutors
- family
- friends
- employers.

....

❛ No, I didn't do this course for the money. I enjoy studying law because it is the right mix of analysis and evaluation for me. I enjoy the intellectual toughness yet real-life grounding of it, and am good at it because I enjoy taking an opinionated stance on the issues. **❜**

JP, SECOND YEAR LAW STUDENT

Higher education advisers and careers advisers can be very helpful for bouncing ideas off, and can put you on the right path to find out reliable information. If you don't have a clue what to study or where you might end up, you could try some questionnaires and quizzes to identify sectors to research in greater detail.

Directgov and UCAS both recommend the **Stamford Test**. This is an online questionnaire about your interests, attitudes and values, which makes broad course suggestions that are dependent on the way you respond to the questions. The objective is to 'present a variety of courses in alignment with your stronger interests.' From these, you may discover several areas for further in-depth investigation. It's easy to understand, quick to fill in, and free to use. Visit:
www.ucas.com/students/choosingcourses/choosingcourse/stamfordtest

Centigrade is another test produced by the same people who created the Stamford test, to help you find up to eight course areas that will suit you best. It is administered for free by some schools, or can be taken online for a £15 fee. It contains 150 questions and the results go into far greater detail than the Stamford Test. Some students find it useful, but others find the process a little 'mechanical' and strange. See:
www.centigradeonline.co.uk

If you're at school or college, you may be able to use **Fast Tomato**. This website has a really useful range of functionality, starting with psychometric questionnaires to help you get ideas about courses, and more, including careers and places to study. It looks at qualifications, and gives you a wide range of suggestions for the future. You can also obtain a free 24-hour pass to use the site, which will give you enough time to use most of the relevant features. See: www.fasttomato.com

When you're filling in questionnaires, don't say what you *think* you should say, just answer honestly about how things really make you feel. It's better if there's nobody looking over your shoulder. The results of these tests are only a jumping-off point to get your imagination going, and you don't have to follow all their suggestions. After that, the hard work really starts!

....

❝ I tried the Stamford Test: it isn't bad, most of it seems to make sense to me. There's no harm in doing it; it's quick and easy, but I wouldn't take it too seriously if you already have an idea of what you want to do. Mine was fairly accurate though. ❞
KATHRYN, AGE 18

WHICH LEVEL OF QUALIFICATION?
The main qualifications covered in this book are full time courses, including the following.

- Three-year undergraduate degree courses leading to Bachelor of Arts, Bachelor of Science or Bachelor of Engineering awards. Most of these are with 'honours' to show the amount of work involved and the high level of specialisation.
- Four-year undergraduate degree courses, such as degrees in Scotland, or sandwich degrees (with a year working in industry), leading to awards such as Bachelor of Arts or Bachelor of Science. These are also usually with honours (some Scottish universities describe these degrees as Master of Arts with honours).
- Two-year foundation courses, which are usually two-year courses (starting at 'year zero') that prepare you for a vocation, or allow you

to gain entry onto a relevant undergraduate degree course upon successful completion.

- Two-year courses leading to Higher National Diploma awards. If completed with high enough grades, this can lead the student into the third year of a degree.

HELP! I CAN'T DECIDE ON MY CAREER AFTER UNI!

Not everyone manages to firmly decide on a potential career at this time, and if that includes you then don't panic. In spite of current money- and employment-related worries, a huge proportion of high-flying graduate jobs don't ask for a particular degree, and some careers, including teaching and journalism, can be entered via a postgraduate diploma.

You could be better off concentrating on looking for a course of study that inspires you academically and plays to your personal strengths, and you may also be able to do a degree or diploma that's relatively general and won't drastically narrow down your career opportunities after graduation. Once you find potential courses you like the look of, then you can concentrate on finding out about the career prospects of graduates from those particular courses.

WHICH SUBJECT AREA? WHAT CAREER?

By now you might have more of an idea about subjects that you want to study in higher education, or preferences for certain types of employment. Take some time to look at both of these, and begin to slowly narrow the field down. Study lots of subject profiles and career profiles to discover whether either approach suggests any appealing courses.

☑ **TIP**

If your main emphasis is on finding a post-graduation career, turn to page 11 of this chapter.

Finding out more about subject areas

Subject profiles can be a straightforward starting point from which to begin some general reading. They provide an overall feel for each general area, and give an overview of the individual courses that are available within each subject. The *Guardian* has useful subject overviews on its website, detailing general course content, skills that studying the subject can give you, and areas of work this can lead to after graduation. Click on the 'More about this subject' link on each page:

www.guardian.co.uk/education/series/university-guide-2011-subjects

You might wish to continue to study a subject you're already familiar with from school, college or evening classes. This has the advantage of being something that you already know you like or are good at, and it's a familiar area that you'd like to pursue in more depth. Otherwise you can choose a subject that's new, or based on an outside interest – there are many courses at university level that you don't get the opportunity to cover at AS or A level.

Applications for most degrees in the UK are made through UCAS, and you can use their website to browse courses by subject area. They also offer entry profiles for many of the courses on their website (look for the 'EP' symbol), and these are written by admissions staff – in addition to general information, they contain advice about what kind of personal qualities, interests and experiences it will be helpful for you to have if you want to study this particular subject or course successfully Visit:

www.ucas.ac.uk/students/choosingcourses/entryrequirements

....

❝ I've applied to study psychology because I studied it at A level and I found the whole thing really interesting: by far the most interesting out of my A level subjects. I can't wait to find out more and study it in more detail. After I've finished my undergraduate studies I think I'd maybe like to go further and get a doctorate in psychology too. Eventually I'm hoping to go on to be something like a forensic psychologist. ❞

ELAINAH GREER, AGE 17

Single or combined subjects?

If you're finding it hard to narrow your preferences down to a single subject, you might consider a course that combines two different subjects. Dual honours degrees are evenly split between two subject areas – often similar subjects, but occasionally quite diverse. You may also find degrees that offer two subjects as major and minor subjects, where 75% of the time and marks come from the major, and 25% from the minor.

If you want to specialise in a certain subject, particularly if you want to go into postgraduate research, you tend to be better off sticking to a single subject so that you can study the whole thing more comprehensively. Be sure to research the career or postgraduate study prospects of particular courses that offer combined subjects.

Finding out more about careers

If you're concerned about life after graduation, in particular careers, there are several useful places to start your search before you move on to researching individual courses. For example, you could try:

- **Fast Tomato**'s website for advice about careers that might suit you, and the qualifications you'll need to get on in your chosen career. Ask your school or college for a login, or apply for a free 24-hour pass at www.fasttomato.com.
- **Cascaid Kudos** is an online questionnaire and careers resource aimed at 13- to 19-year-olds. The database contains hundreds of different job titles and is updated three times per year. If you're over 19 they have another resource called **Adult Directions** that you can use. You can find them at www.cascaid.com.
- The **Prospects Planner** from Graduate Prospects – a tool that allows you to look at what would motivate you in a job, identify your skills, generate job ideas, and explore jobs in greater detail. It is mainly aimed at undergraduates but can also be used by pre-university students. Click on the 'What jobs would suit me?' link on the main Jobs and Work Experience page to launch the application, at www.prospects.ac.uk/jobs_and_work_experience.htm.
- The **Options with your subject** database. Graduate Prospects also have plenty of advice about careers that you can enter if you're thinking

about studying a broad subject area already. Try their database to see where certain subjects could lead you after graduation, at www.prospects.ac.uk/options_with_your_subject.htm.

- **Directgov** has some more general career profiles too as part of its Next Step service, although not all of the jobs it suggests will require undergraduate study. It's still worth a look if you're gathering ideas, and it contains handy job market information at https://nextstep.direct.gov.uk/planningyourcareer/jobprofiles/Pages/default.aspx.
- Careersoft's **Job Explorer** database is another option for you to consider, with information about jobs, wages, qualifications, similar jobs and careers progression. You can find it at www.careersoft.co.uk/Products/Job_Explorer_Database.

Your nearest careers adviser or careers library should also be able to lend you more detailed books about different careers that you like the sound of, and can advise you about the qualifications needed to work in them. They can also point you in the direction of specific official websites, information agencies and professional bodies.

After this, you can move on to exploring different courses and locations, to see whether they'd suit your personal preferences. As part of this research you will probably want to take note of each individual course's graduate prospects – there's more about this on page 17, along with information about course costs and financing your studies.

‘ Am I worried about prospects after graduating? Maybe I am, but I think that there's always something out there for you and you have to keep trying, even if you have to move to another part of the UK or even go abroad. Sooner or later you will find something that's right for you, even if you have to take a 'not perfect' job to keep you going while you're looking for the one you really want. ’

ANONYMOUS STUDENT, AGE 19

EXPLORING COURSES IN GREATER DEPTH

To see the full range of available course titles in the UK, you can try the following services:

- **UCAS** provides a list of all full-time courses at universities and colleges in the UK that use its admissions service. To find out more, visit www.ucas.com and use the Course Search function. This database is searchable by subjects or course codes, and then you have the option to narrow your search by region, institution and type of course.
- The same full range of course listings is also found in the UCAS *Big Guide for Entry to University or College*, which contains the complete entry requirements for each one.
- Other sources of similar information include *Heap 2012: University Degree Course Offers* and *Choosing Your Degree Course and University*, both by Brian Heap (published by Trotman).
- **Foundation degrees** are listed at the following web address: http://fd.ucas.com/CourseSearch/Default.aspx.
- **Course Discover** is the searchable database of UK higher education courses mentioned earlier in this chapter. This subscription service is available via careers advisers or local libraries. In addition to the academic information, it contains a wide range of useful data including work placement opportunities and faculty information. Go to http://demo.coursediscoveronline.co.uk/a_about-home.asp.
- For part-time degrees and diplomas you can visit HotCourses at www.hotcourses.com.
- Some extra music courses can be found via the **CUKAS** website. You can search by instrument, course type or conservatoire, at www.cukas.ac.uk/students/coursesearch.
- **The UK Department for Business Innovation and Skills** (BIS) runs a website of recognised UK degrees that you may wish to check with, at www.dcsf.gov.uk/recogniseddegrees.
- **The British Council** also provides a complete listing of all official courses at universities and colleges in the UK via its website, at www.educationuk.org. This may be useful if you're applying to the UK from overseas.

You then need to look thoroughly at the content and format of each potentially suitable course, to see whether it will interest you and suit your learning preferences and career aspirations. At this point, given the general state of the economy, it's also a good idea to look at financial implications and employment prospects. You should also carefully study the entry requirements for the courses that appeal to you the most, to gauge your chances of making successful applications to any of them.

COURSE CONTENT AND FORMAT

The content of a course, and the way it's organised and taught, can vary greatly. In fact, two courses with the same name may completely differ according to the institution where they're being taught. Differences in content and format can make you love or hate a course, so pick with care. Consider which topics are likely to catch your eye and which ones might send you to sleep, and which course format you'll respond to the best.

There's no national curriculum for undergraduate courses, so they differ according to staff and location. For this reason, it's vital to find out exactly what you could be getting yourself into with every single course you're considering. University and college websites and prospectuses often contain comprehensive information, including course content, teaching format and assessment methods. You can also contact the institutions directly by phone or email to ask for more details. They may be able to supply you with extra course brochures as well.

Courses that use the UCAS service may have a wide range of data included in their entry profiles on the UCAS website. Entry profiles may contain a list of required qualifications and personal characteristics, and a description of the institution's entry criteria. Some entry profiles are more complete than others, and some courses have no entry profile at all, in which case you may decide to contact the institution directly.

During the application process you will need to demonstrate knowledge of what the course contains, and how it's likely to be taught – this shows admissions staff that you're interested and motivated, and that your expectations of the course are realistic.

What should you consider with course content?

- Sub-topics on the syllabus you're especially interested in
- Sub-topics you really can't stand

- Areas you could excel in
- Areas where you may need extra support or study
- Opportunities to specialise or gain work experience
- The way the format changes throughout the years of the degree
- How course content might relate to future careers

What should you consider with course formats?

- Methods of teaching and learning you respond to best
- Whether the course is modular or non-modular
- Flexibility (whether some parts are optional or compulsory)
- How much independent study is required
- The level of support from teaching staff
- The number of hours of lectures, seminars and practicals per week
- The time spent on work placement
- What key transferable skills you will learn
- How the course is assessed: essays, reviews, presentations, projects, exams, continuous assessment
- How the marking structure is weighted

SANDWICH COURSES

Many degree and Higher National Diploma courses are now being offered in the 'sandwich' format, which includes years of study at college combined with a year or more in industry, commerce or the social sector. Students earn a wage while they're working on placement, and may also gain sponsorship and go on to a full-time job with their placement firms when they graduate. Common formats include:

- the 'thick sandwich': two years at college, followed by a year in industry, followed by a final year in college
- a 1:3:1 course: one year in industry, three (or even four) years of study, and a final year at a work placement
- a 'thin sandwich': the arrangement varies, but involves two six-month work placements, interspersed with time at college.

If you think this format might be right for you, details on all sandwich courses can be gained from the UCAS website (www.ucas.com) or from university websites and prospectuses.

CAREER PROSPECTS AND FINANCIAL IMPLICATIONS

As the cost of studying rises and several sectors of the economy are struggling, many potential students have become increasingly worried about running up debts and finding a good job at the end of their course.

With this in mind, there are several things to consider when looking at specific courses:

- Whether a course is vocational or non-vocational
- Drop-out rates (see page 27)
- Graduate employment rates and types by department/course
- Graduate salaries by subject
- Graduate job market situation
- General graduate recruitment patterns by institution (see Chapter 3)
- Course fees and tuition fees
- Accommodation costs and general cost of living
- Funding/loans/bursaries/sponsorship etc.

Vocational or non-vocational course?

Vocational degrees such as dentistry, medicine and veterinary medicine have become even more popular in recent years as applicants are attracted by specific work-related training, and possibly high salaries or greater job security. Similarly, some applicants fear taking a non-vocational degree because it may be harder to get a graduate job initially. This is because candidates may not appear to have the precise skills that an employer is looking for, or because there is more competition for each vacancy. However, over 40% of graduate jobs are open to graduates from any discipline, so it isn't all doom and gloom. In addition, taking any course you excel in vastly increases your chances of gaining a First – which can open many doors for you, regardless of subject. Ask a careers adviser about vocational and non-vocational degrees if you are having difficulty deciding.

❛ If you have chosen a subject or course to study but have not chosen a career path, remember that a lot of graduate level jobs are open to graduates of any discipline. It is important to separate out vocational and non-vocational degrees. For example, taking a degree in music won't necessarily lead to work in this area, however it will give you many transferable skills. Another way is to research the employment destinations of graduates from subjects you are interested in. Take a look at the data on www. prospects.ac.uk and www.unistats.com. This is a complex decision and is also related to knowledge of the labour market and employment pattern; it would be prudent to ask for a guidance interview in addition to personal research. **❜**

NAOMI ELFRED, CONNEXIONS PERSONAL ADVISER

Graduate employment rates and types by department/course

It's relatively easy to find reliable statistics for university departments to find out how many of their graduates end up in graduate jobs within six months of completing their course, and the top ten types of employment for graduates of a particular subject. You can also find out how many of them are in further education, combining work with further study, or who are coyly described as 'presumed unemployed'. This Destinations of Leavers from Higher Education (DLHE) data can be found arranged by institution and by subject at the Unistats website (www.unistats.com). Be advised that this does not give statistics for individual courses.

To find out graduate employment rates on a particular course, look it up on UCAS Course Search and you should find percentages of students employed within six months of graduating, the types of work they've gone into, and names of major employers who take on graduates. If this information isn't listed, contact the department directly for more advice.

Graduate salaries by subject

For a quick and easy reference to average graduate earnings by subject studied, see the most recent 'What do graduates earn?' table at The Complete University

Guide website. This contains HESA data, and is arranged in order of high to low earnings. Visit:
www.thecompleteuniversityguide.co.uk/single.htm?ipg=6370

Graduate job market situation

General trends in the graduate job market can be found in the latest Graduate Recruitment Survey from the Association of Graduate Recruiters (AGR) at www. agr.org.uk, and the most recent Graduate Market Employment Survey from Highfliers at www.highfliers.co.uk. This can help you to consider areas of work that are likely to see increased levels of recruitment or continuing graduate employment, as well as research minimum entry requirements for jobs and starting salaries.

It is also worth contacting a careers adviser or Connexions for more advice about graduate recruitment patterns in subjects that you're considering.

Course fees and tuition fees

Look up a specific course in UCAS Course Search and click on the 'Fees, bursaries and financial support' link. This should take you to a separate page which details course fees for home, EU and international students, tuition fees, and extra considerations such as fees for placements and years abroad. If this information is incomplete or out of date, go to the university website and search for the information there. If this doesn't yield results, contact the department or faculty directly. Keep in mind that you may not have to pay the entire stated course fee or tuition fee as many exemptions can apply.

....

I've realised that I'm not that worried about money, even though I don't come from a well-off family. Think about it – you will be able to borrow money at the lowest interest rate you will ever be offered for the rest of your life. Loans and bursaries and other money are easier to qualify for and arrange than people make out. I'd say don't let it put you off applying if you don't come from a rich family; don't miss out on a university education. 〟

ANONYMOUS STUDENT

Accommodation costs and general cost of living

Course Discover is available via careers advisers or local libraries. In addition to the academic course information, it includes course-specific financial information and a new tool called the Ready Money Reckoner, to help you work out accommodation costs, your likely yearly expenditure, and the local cost of living. See: http://demo.coursediscoveronline.co.uk/a_about-home.asp

Other sources of information include university and student union websites, and books such as *The Guide to Student Money 2011* by Gwenda Thomas (published by Trotman) or *The Complete University Guide: Student Finance* by Bernard Kingston and Nicola Chalton (published by Right Way).

Funding/loans/bursaries/sponsorship etc.

Individual UCAS Course Search pages contain information about bursaries and scholarships that are available for specific courses. They also contain links to each university's website for further funding information. You can look here for details of exemptions, grants and benefits. Also try reading the latest edition of *University Scholarships, Awards and Bursaries* by Brian Heap (published by Trotman) for a comprehensive guide to universities and colleges offering extra financial support, sponsorships, and awards offered by professional, commercial and other organisations.

The funding and tuition fees landscape changes regularly, but you can keep abreast of it at Hotcourses Student Money (www.scholarship-search. org.uk), and Directgov (www.direct.gov.uk/en/EducationAndLearning/ UniversityAndHigherEducation/StudentFinance/index.htm).

ENTRY REQUIREMENTS

When you compare entry requirements for courses with similar titles and content, there is much variation between institutions. This variation should mainly be considered as a mark of relative popularity; the higher education entry process essentially functions as a market and the grades represent supply and demand. By raising entry requirements an oversubscribed institution hopes to be less swamped with applications, and by lowering requirements an under-subscribed institution hopes to increase its annual influx of applications and fill its course.

Degree course offers can make or break your applications. For every course you're considering applying to, you must go through the entry requirements as thoroughly as possible to make sure that you meet them. In addition to being asked for certain grades or points at A and AS level, you may also have to have high grades at GCSE in subjects such as maths or English, or to produce certificates to prove you have been vaccinated against certain infections or that you have no criminal convictions, and so on. It's all about reading the small print – failing to meet any of the compulsory requirements, however minor it might seem at the time, will make you ineligible for consideration and your application will automatically be declined, wasting one or more of your possible chances to get onto a course.

It's important to know that university and college departments can re-adjust their average offers at any time – they all reserve the right to do this in the small print of their applications information, and it's perfectly legal for them to do so.

MID-CYCLE CHANGES TO ENTRY REQUIREMENTS

During 2010, it was noticed that several university departments had taken the unusual step of changing their entry requirements in the middle of the applications cycle (previously they would have waited until the start of the following cycle to make these changes). The institutions included Cambridge, Newcastle, Nottingham and York. This mid-cycle change was due to unusually high numbers of applicants to certain courses, and the end result was that more points were needed in order for applicants to be considered. The average change was one grade higher than the original total: for example A*AA changed to A*A*A.

It caused concern and shock because people had already started applying, believing that the entry requirements were slightly lower. Some of the people who'd applied after carefully studying the original entry requirements realised that they would probably not meet these new requirements, and had perhaps 'wasted' some or all of their choices and thus jeopardised their chances. Many schools protested that the changes were unfair and could deny applicants places at their chosen universities, although some universities replied that the earlier applicants would be judged according to the original criteria and would therefore not lose out. Unfortunately there is no way to predict whether there will be a similar situation this year.

How can you prevent this situation from affecting you?

- Do your research thoroughly and check entry criteria once again on the day that you submit your application.
- Some schools advise that applicants should print out a copy of course entry criteria on the day that they apply, to keep as evidence.
- Apply to universities that require a range of grades. In your five choices, you could have a selection of upper, middle and lower minimum entry requirements, based around the grades that you hope to get. Doing this might provide you with a safety net in case the universities do make offers that are higher than the minimum entry requirements.
- Learn more about UCAS Extra (see Chapter 7) and Clearing (see Chapter 8) in case you don't get a suitable offer.
- Get more advice from careers advisers and Connexions if you're still worried.

Entry requirements may also include essays written for admissions tutors, submission of portfolio or recent coursework, and the results of admissions tests and interviews. These are detailed in Chapter 6.

What are the entry requirements for my course?

This varies from place to place and course to course. You may be asked for an overall set of grades at A level (such as AAB or CCC), or you may be required to attain certain marks in specific exams.

UCAS also operates a tariff system, which aims to allow the comparison of different types of qualifications, and puts a numerical value to levels and 'volumes' (amounts) of achievement. Universities and colleges are then able to use the UCAS Tariff to make comparisons between applicants with different qualifications.

According to UCAS, the Tariff works in the following way:

- Points can be aggregated from the different qualifications included in the Tariff.

- There is no ceiling to the number of points which can be accumulated.
- There is no double counting – applicants cannot count the same or similar qualifications twice.
- Certain qualifications within the Tariff build on qualifications in the same subject. In these cases only the qualification with the higher Tariff score will be counted. For example, AS points will be subsumed into the A level points for the same subject. The same principle applies to Scottish Highers and Advanced Highers, key skills and music awards at different levels or grades.
- Although Tariff points can be accumulated in a variety of ways, not all of these will necessarily be acceptable for entry to a particular course.

To find out more, and to view the tariff system and tariff tables, visit www.ucas.com/students/ucas_tariff.

For entry into some higher education courses, you may be able to use accreditation of prior learning (APL). It is the recognition of, and award of, academic credit on the basis of demonstrated learning (not just experience) that has occurred at some time in the past. There are different ways to calculate APL, so you are advised to check with individual course tutors if you think you might qualify.

Finding out about entry requirements

You can begin your research by looking at one of two books. The UCAS *Big Guide* is a book plus CD-ROM that contains complete entry requirements for all UK higher education courses using the UCAS tariff. Their website (www.ucas.com) also contains expanded entry profiles which explain more about the type of university or college, what the course entails and so on. *Heap 2012: University Degree Course Offers* by Brian Heap (published by Trotman) is a comprehensive guide to entry requirements that uses official information. It lists target grades and tariff points needed to gain entry to all UK courses, and also mentions teaching quality, research ratings, number of applicants per place (see below), graduate prospects, plus subject-specific advice for personal statements and interviews.

While both of these guides are well respected, comprehensive and regularly updated, remember that university and college departments can re-adjust their average offers at any time, so don't assume you'll be made exactly the same offers as in the books. It is wise to keep checking the UCAS website and university websites to make sure that the requirements haven't changed.

Applicants per place

In addition to high entry grades, the number of applicants for each place on a course will help you to gauge how competitive it might be. It varies considerably from institution to institution, according to how popular the course (or perhaps the overall university) is. Don't be too put off if your favourite course has many applicants per place – if you know you can get the grades and you have the right personality then you've got to at least give it a try. Some applicants will pick one or more courses from their five options that aren't quite so competitive, as insurance. You can find out the number of applicants per place at specific universities by using UCAS's applications data on their website, or on specific courses by using *Heap 2012: University Degree Course Offers* by Brian Heap (published by Trotman) or UCAS's *Progression to . . .* series of subject guides.

Being realistic

While it's good to be ambitious, it's important not to apply to too many colleges and universities where you're unlikely to meet their conditions at exam time, in case you don't get in at all. Most applicants include at least one institution on their entry form that asks for lower grades or points, just in case exam results don't go according to plan, and also often include a choice where they're aiming slightly higher.

If your predicted grades are not high enough to get onto the courses you most want to study, your main options are:

A Take a chance and apply to at least one anyway (bearing in mind that competitive courses might not consider you), pick an insurance choice with lower entry requirements, then work as hard as you can to get the grades.

B Wait until you've sat your exams, then – if you get the grades – apply through Clearing or for the following academic year (possibly taking a gap year in between). This can be risky so think about how much risk you're prepared to take.

C Reconsider your choices and perhaps apply to the same course at institutions with lower entry requirements, or apply to other courses that are related or different to increase your chances of getting in.

For option C, be aware that if you accept a place on one of the courses with lower entry requirements via UCAS, then get higher grades than expected, you may still be bound by UCAS rules to attend the course that you originally accepted. In some circumstances you can become eligible to use Adjustment, where your original place is kept safe but you have a short period to look for courses with higher entry requirements. If you decide to go for a different course with higher entry requirements via Clearing, you will have to request the original institution to release you from your obligation. This can take time, and during this period all suitable Clearing places may become filled. For more about the pros and cons, see Chapter 8.

Only you can decide what to do, but take plenty of advice before following any specific course of action.

IMPROVING YOUR CHANCES

Once you have seen courses that interest you, and looked at their entry profiles and requirements, turn your thoughts to how you can attract the attention of admissions tutors and give your application the edge over the competition. Here are a few suggestions:

- Are entry requirements high, but you think you're in with a chance of meeting them? Let this motivate you to give even more attention to getting your grades if you're taking A levels, AS levels or equivalents. If your predicted grades aren't great, and you think you can do better, do whatever you can to prove them wrong – higher grades can get you onto a top quality degree course during clearing, for example.
- If you haven't done too well in mock exams so far, and you have extenuating circumstances such as a bereavement or long period of illness, make sure this is made clear when you send off applications. A supporting letter from a tutor, or a sympathetic reference stating your real potential, can be a great help.
- Use course profiles to find out favoured personal characteristics and so on, then work out how you can demonstrate these characteristics on an application form or personal statement. For example, if you need to appear numerate, you could perhaps mention working as a cashier during summer holidays. To appear compassionate, you could arrange to do some volunteering or fundraising, and so on. You can also consider leadership

awards, or joining schemes such as The Duke of Edinburgh's Award to improve your profile, but do remember that these can take up a lot of time.

- If you haven't done so already, arrange relevant work experience, work shadowing, or even short visits to places of employment, especially if you're hoping to do a vocational degree. Make notes on what makes up an average working day, what might be challenging, and so on. Use it as a chance to ask lots of questions, and to make sure it isn't a profession you'd find unbearably dull or unpleasant.
- Some taster schemes, summer schools, extra credit courses for sixth formers, and the Open University Young Applicants in Schools and Colleges short courses can really make your application stand out.
- Be on the lookout for 'partner schemes' at nearby universities. If you meet their criteria, such as low family income, certain institutions may slightly lower their entry requirements for you.

‎Newcastle is my first choice as it has a really good reputation, it's well respected (red-brick) and has great graduate prospects. It's also, out of the three local universities, the one I liked the feel of the most while I was there. I also found out that because I am from a lower-income family, I qualify for something called the Partners Scheme, which means I can get a lower offer if I complete a two-week summer school. This kind of sealed the deal for me, as I really want to go there and this makes it even more possible. My predicted grades are AAB, which is what Newcastle would have required without the Partners Scheme, but I chose to do Partners in order to lower it to BBC just because I wouldn't like to miss out over a few marks or something.

LIZZIE JOBES, AGE 20, SOUTH TYNESIDE COLLEGE

NEWER SUBJECTS AND COURSES

In the last few years a diverse range of new subjects has appeared at degree and diploma level. They may be specific to emerging career paths, such as the renewable energy industry, or catering to specialist educational interests, such as rare languages. It could put you at an advantage in a certain employment sector when you graduate, but beware of the 'teething troubles' with teaching methods, assessment and new curricula that can also plague new courses. These newer options might not be on the radar of some careers officers, so you must be prepared to do a lot of independent research if you're considering applying.

ACADEMIC STANDARDS AND QUALITY

'Academic standards' refers to how hard it is to gain a particular standard of degree (e.g. a First, a 2.i, a 2.ii, etc.) at a college or university. Ideally, these standards should be similar across all the different UK institutions, even though their course content may vary. 'Academic quality' refers to how well courses are taught and assessed, and how well the students are supported.

The Quality Assurance Agency for Higher Education (QAA) advises UK higher education providers on both academic standards and academic quality. It provides external quality assurance in addition to the universities' own internal review mechanisms. Potential students will be most interested in the QAA's Institutional Review Reports. These contain summaries of institutional and subject-level management, looking at areas of strengths and weaknesses. Further details can be found on their website at www.qaa.ac.uk.

The Teaching Quality Information website was replaced by the **Unistats** website (www.unistats.com) in November 2007. This new site is owned by HEFCE (the Higher Education Funding Council for England) and run by UCAS and HotCourses to help potential students and their advisers compare subjects (but not individual courses) at universities and colleges in the UK. The information is provided by HESA (Higher Education Statistics Agency), the FE data service, and the National Student Survey (run by HEFCE).

It includes information on the following, searchable by subject and university.

- Student data: entry qualifications and UCAS points, continuation and achievement
- Destinations of Leavers from Higher Education (DLHE) data: destinations of leavers, job categories and job types
- Context statistics: student domicile, age, level of study, gender and study mode
- National Student Survey and student satisfaction

☑ **TIP**

Reading up on a college or university's academic quality and academic standards can help you put together some intelligent questions to ask during open days or admissions interviews.

While government league tables exist for English primary and secondary schools, there are no such official classifications for higher education institutions. Some newspapers and other organisations produce their own league tables, but each one is based on different criteria and they rarely agree with one another. They can be useful to gain a wider picture, particularly when choosing which institution to study at, but should not be the sole basis for decision-making. The league tables are covered in greater detail in Chapter 3 of this book.

RESEARCH RATINGS

Some people think that if a college or university produces excellent research, this attracts top quality staff and provides a cutting-edge learning environment for undergraduates. Others take the view that research staff may not necessarily be gifted teaching staff, or may not be able to devote much time to helping undergraduates. Research ratings do matter if you're thinking about going into research after completing an undergraduate degree, but otherwise they may not be the deciding factor in picking the right course for you.

The Research Assessment Exercise (RAE) takes place every few years to judge the quality of research being carried out in UK colleges and universities. The current assessment is the 2008 edition, and the last complete set of statistics is from 2001. The results can be obtained from www.rae.ac.uk.

DROP-OUTS, SUCCESS AND SATISFACTION

Everyone wants to be on a course where they are likely to be motivated, happy and successful. Is it possible to gauge these variables?

Drop-out rates

Financial problems have been given as the main reason for students dropping out of university in recent years, but students sometimes leave their courses because they're unhappy with the course content or the way it's organised and taught. Therefore these figures should be read with caution, and preferably combined with levels of student satisfaction, as they don't tell the whole story. To look them up, search for 'continuation rates' data on www.unistats.com. This will tell you how many students completed their course, how many left with no award, and how many are 'dormant' (the website has more information on this).

Success (a.k.a. degree class and progression)

In this instance, 'success' means the number of students who passed their degree, and how many of them gained top classes of degree (i.e. First and 2.i). This can be a measure of the calibre of the student intake, a measure of good teaching and student support, or occasionally it's a sign that the course is too easy. These figures should probably be viewed in combination with the entry grades a course requires, QAA ratings, and student satisfaction.

Satisfaction

The National Student Survey results are also available on www.unistats.com and they make for interesting reading. The main figure they provide is the percentage of students who say that they're satisfied with the quality of their course. The survey is also broken down into areas of finer detail, mentioning teaching standards, assessment and feedback, academic support, course organisation, learning resources and personal development.

DEFERMENT/GAP YEAR

Around 7% of all accepted first year undergraduates request to defer starting their course for one year. Some people want a break from the pressures of studying, and others want the opportunity to explore the world around them while they're not tied down with jobs and mortgages. Other students use it to gain vital work experience that could give them the edge when they're applying for courses or future employment, and others are simply working to save up money so that they can fund their higher education.

A gap year can have a positive or negative effect depending upon where you're planning to study afterwards. Tutors on longer courses, such as architecture, sometimes think that it causes too much delay, whereas others think it allows students to develop more maturity, skills and confidence. This varies widely from department to department and even from tutor to tutor, so if you're considering a gap year you should discuss it with staff at the universities you're applying to, preferably well in advance. Ask whether there are any activities they especially value, such as extra learning, volunteering or specific types of work experience.

If you're considering having a gap year, think about how you're going to apply for a place at university or college. You can apply for deferred entry so that you already know you're coming back to start a degree at the end of the gap year – this has the advantage of you being able to work closely with your school during the application period. Or you can apply to university during your gap year for entry that academic year – this has the advantage of you knowing your grades already so you don't have the uncertainty of waiting for conditional offers. University departments have their own preferences on this too, so check with them first.

☑ TIP

Remember that universities are not obliged to accept your request for deferment. Do your research, and if in doubt, play it safe.

A fruitful gap year takes some planning, especially if you're hoping to travel. You can make your own arrangements or join schemes where much of the organisation is done for you. Students often combine activities during the year rather than sticking to one thing, so they may spend some of the time being 'productive' (working, volunteering, learning) and some of the time being more leisurely (travelling, socialising, etc.).

You can start your research by:

- finding a nearby gap year fair at www.yearoutgroup.org/calendar.htm
- talking to a Connexions adviser about your options
- learning about gap perks and pitfalls on www.gapadvice.org
- chatting to other gap year students or arranging a trip on www.gapyear.com
- learning about Year in Industry opportunities at www.yini.org.uk/students.php
- reading *Your Gap Year* by Susan Griffith (published by Vacation Work), or *The Gap Year Guidebook* by Alison Withers (published by John Catt Ltd).

SUMMARY: COURSE CHOICE TIPS

1. Invest the time. Be prepared to do a lot of research if you're looking for the right course, as there are so many variables and lots of different resources you need to use to look up all the information. There's plenty of data available, but it isn't all found in the same place.

2. It's all about you. Make sure that your course will fire your imagination and hold your interest, and make the best of your skills, talents and personality. Bounce your ideas off a wide range of people, make lists, and take personality quizzes.

3. Start looking ahead. You are able to find out what your career prospects might be if you study a particular subject at a particular university. You can look at employment levels, and what types of jobs previous students have gone on to. You can also start by looking at jobs that might suit you, then finding the right courses to gain entry to those careers.

4. Don't panic if you don't have a career in mind. You may end up picking a subject that interests you, and taking it from there. You can also collect subject- and course-related data to see what careers a course could lead you into, so don't worry too much at this stage.

5. Explore costs and funding opportunities. As it becomes ever more expensive to put yourself through higher education, students need to consider additional sources of funding from loans, grants, bursaries, paid work experience and more. You should also factor in university fees, course costs, and local cost of living for each course to help you make a budget.

6. Course content is key. Two courses with the same name can contain very different topics and sub-topics. Be prepared to go into the finer detail when you're looking at what you might be learning about.

7. Pick the right mode of study. Only you can decide what course structure, teaching style, and amount of student-directed learning will suit you best. Again, it comes down to thoroughly researching your options and reading the course information's small print.

8. Use official data. Make sure you're doing a recognised course leading to an official qualification, and check out ratings for academic standards and quality. You may also wish to see research ratings, and read the results of the National Student Survey. You can also ask around for opinions, but don't rely too much on anecdotal information.

9. What grades are needed? You must balance optimism with realism when looking at course entry requirements – don't set your expectations too low, but at the same time consider what other options you might have if you don't get the grades you were hoping for.

10. What does 'success' mean to you? Whether it's completing your studies without dropping out, getting a first, getting a graduate job quickly afterwards, or simply being happy with the teaching and organisation of your course and what you're learned from it, there are different ways to gauge how successful you might be.

CHAPTER TWO

COMMON MISCONCEPTIONS ABOUT COURSES

 y now, you might have a fairly firm idea of the subject, or subjects, you'd like to study. Once you reach the stage of looking at individual courses it's essential that you continue reading and researching, and don't lose your focus. Course titles, course structure and content, and qualifications needed to enter certain careers are of crucial importance, and your applications must show that you've read the small print and understood it. Avoid making assumptions or skimming over the details – it's easy to make mistakes and you truly need to know exactly what you're letting yourself in for.

⸻

'The content and structure of degrees vary so much between unis. English is a prime example. If the head of department has a specialist interest you need to check that the programme of study is not overly biased to this. If they offer a sandwich degree are you responsible for work placements? Also remember that we all have our individual learning style preferences, so it's important that students understand how they will be taught. In medicine, for example, teaching methods and clinical contact can vary enormously between unis. **'**

FRASER SHADWELL, CONNEXIONS PERSONAL ADVISER

GENERAL MISCONCEPTIONS

Attention to detail is key when you are choosing between courses and selecting your favourite ones. Names and entry requirements can be confusing, and courses that superficially appear to be identical may well turn out to have little in common. Your personal preferences for course content and format, teaching style and modes of assessment make big a difference too, and can strongly affect your enjoyment of your studies. Make sure there are no nasty hidden surprises.

Entry requirements and average offers

Many applicants assume that you can tell the quality of a course simply by looking at the target offers that are made to applicants. However, this is a mistake. On their own, entry requirements say nothing specific about the course content or the teaching quality. The average target offer represents the popularity of a course more than anything else – higher education is a market, and the more popular courses raise their entry requirements so that they don't get swamped with too many applicants. The popularity of a course can come from the overall academic reputation of a university or college, or a department within it, rather than anything related to that particular course.

The average conditional offers for courses are listed on websites and in a variety of guidebooks (see Chapter 1). Remember that they are just guidelines, and are usually based on the previous year's figures – which can change over time. If a university or college really like you, they could make you an unconditional offer anyway, or sometimes they will make you a conditional offer that asks you to obtain slightly lower grades.

Entry requirements may also be stated in points as part of a comparative overview, but in reality not all institutions use tariff points to gauge the potential of their applicants. Carefully research the entry criteria of any and all of the courses that you might apply to, as sometimes they are less straightforward than you might think. It's not always as simple as obtaining 'BBB' in your A levels, which is how it could appear in a table – you might need a minimum grade in a specific subject, or to have done very well in particular GCSEs first.

Confusion over course names

Course names also trip plenty of applicants up. Many have similar spellings in their titles but can land you in entirely different careers: for example, pharmacology is not the same as pharmacy, and will not help you to train as a pharmacist. Be extra careful not to mix up courses with similar-sounding names, or to confuse course variations. There may also be specific words in a course title that give students the incorrect impression, so it's quite common for people to confuse a course such as theatre studies with gaining a performing arts place at drama school, and so on.

As always, reading through all the provided course information is necessary to dispel any myths or misleading ideas. Extra research also helps to create a more realistic picture, and asking the university questions when you get stuck is the perfect way to deal with confusion that might arise while you're reading their literature. Only ask when you get stuck though, as university staff can be extremely busy at certain times of year and might not take too kindly to being asked questions that you could have easily found out about by yourself. On the other hand, a few searching, intelligent questions can make a good impression as it suggests you're focused and interested.

General course details

Some people jump to the conclusion that courses with the same name are the same everywhere you go, but they'd be wrong. General course details are highly variable, and they can lead to students loving their courses or hating them and even dropping out. It's simply not something you can hope to second guess, so you must research the course content thoroughly and be clear about what you're applying for.

Your personal preferences are vital to consider when you're looking at degrees and other courses. What do you respond to best? Here's a checklist to run through for every course you're seriously considering:

- **Course structure.** Is this a course that's split into discrete modules, or is it something more traditional and continuous? What do the major components consist of? Do you like the look of all of them and could you do well in them? Which subtopics are given the most weight on this course? How does the structure change over the years of study?
- **Course type.** Is the course being offered as single or dual honours? Are there major and minor subjects? Would you be expected to follow one subject closely, or study something broader and more multidisciplinary?
- **Career considerations.** This area is a deal-breaker for many students. Does the course comply with the regulations of the appropriate

professional bodies? Are you certain that this the qualification you must have to get into your chosen career? Is this qualification needed before you can pursue a particular postgraduate course or other qualification?

- **Work experience opportunities or chance to travel abroad.** Is this optional or compulsory, and what do other students say about it? What's available to choose from? Where are you willing to go?
- **Teaching style.** How many lectures are there per week, and how long is each one? Which staff do the lecturing? How much do they interact with the students? Are there seminars, tutorials, other presentations, guest speakers and so on? What other teaching methods are used?
- **Self-directed learning.** To what extent are students responsible for their own reading and research, and how many hours are allowed in the timetable for this? Do you like being left to take charge of your own learning or do you prefer more guidance from staff? What support is provided to students to assist their self-directed learning?
- **Flexibility.** Can you take on extra subjects or drop some? What's compulsory? Do you actively dislike any compulsory subjects or modules that are listed? Is there room for specialisation later on during the course? Can you study additional topics that aren't related to your main subject?
- **Modes of assessment.** Is it continuous assessment or mainly exam-based? What format do exams take and when are they held? What proportion of marks are given for essays, practicals, reviews, presentations, work experience assessments, dissertations, and so on? Do you do better in exams or would you do anything to avoid them?

SUBJECT-SPECIFIC MISCONCEPTIONS

If you haven't read the prospectuses carefully enough, it's easy to get the wrong idea about a subject. Be careful, as this can easily be spotted on your application by admissions staff, or trip you up during an important interview. Here are some common sources of confusion:

Animal care

This course does not qualify you to work as a vet or veterinary nurse.

Architecture

This course is more about design, rather than engineering.

Aviation

Will not turn you into a pilot or air traffic controller.

Biomedical sciences

This course does not qualify graduates to practise as medical doctors or nurses.

Building

Does not train students to become bricklayers or structural engineers.

Economics

This is not the same as taking a business studies course.

Education studies

Graduates of this course are not qualified to work as teachers.

Film studies

This is not a course that trains budding film-makers (it teaches analysis rather than practical techniques).

Food science

This is not for someone who wants to train to become a chef.

Forestry

Does not train applicants to become lumberjacks.

History of art

Students are not expected to produce their own artworks.

Languages

Applied language courses are not about the study of literature.

Media studies

Will not train applicants for a specific job in the media, or to be journalists.

Music

This degree is not necessarily about being a performer.

Pharmacology and pharmaceutical science

This is not a pharmacy degree and will not qualify a graduate to work as a pharmacist.

Physiotherapy

This is not all about treating sports injuries.

Podiatry

An academic course, which is more complicated than becoming a chiropodist or pedicurist.

Psychology

Does not train students to become psychotherapists or psychiatrists.

Radiography

Not to be confused with radiotherapy or radio production.

Religious studies

Not necessarily about Christianity or any other specific religion, and does not qualify you to work as a priest.

Social and public policy and administration

Doesn't provide students with a qualification in social work.

Sports sciences

Not a course for training Olympic hopefuls or other athletes.

Theatre studies

These courses should not be confused with scriptwriting, stage school or performing arts courses.

Zoology

Not the same as Veterinary Medicine or Veterinary Science.

SUMMARY: SEVEN STEPS TO UNDERSTANDING COURSE INFORMATION

1. Keep focused. Attention to detail makes all the difference when you're looking for the right course, and making an application to one. Picking the right subject is only the beginning.

2. Read ALL of the small print. You don't just need some understanding, you need complete understanding of the important points. This helps at interview too.

3. Don't jump to conclusions. Not all courses are the same, even if they appear superficially similar, and you'll only find out by putting the groundwork in. A popular course with high entry standards isn't necessarily the 'best' course either.

4. Take care with titles. Similar titles can lead to entirely different degrees, qualifications and careers. Check spellings and key words.

5. Respect entry requirements. Make sure you meet all compulsory requirements for your application, or you'll run the risk of getting immediately rejected.

6. Course details do matter. Content, format, teaching style and marking schemes vary widely between institutions. Your preferences are important, and can make the difference between thriving and being unhappy.

7. Keep asking questions. If thorough research doesn't give you the answers you need, don't be scared to ask university staff any further questions you have. It also makes you look motivated. However, remember it's not a good idea to hog admissions officers' time by asking questions that you could easily have answered yourself during your research.

CHAPTER THREE

CHOOSING YOUR INSTITUTION

Where to study can be just as important as what to study. If you're an undergraduate you could be spending three, four or five years at the university or college of your choice, and you might as well enjoy it! Whether you're looking for top graduate prospects, historical surroundings, a low cost of living or a busy entertainment scene, there's something for everyone. The more you can find out now, the better your chances of finding the perfect location will be.

....

' Your choice of higher education institution really is important. For most people university is also much more than just gaining a degree, and choices should be made on a wider basis. For example, what social activities are they offering? If you require learning support how is this delivered? Finally, geography is a key consideration. How far do you want to be away from home, and is it campus-based or urban? **'**

NIKKI BRUNNING, CONNEXIONS PERSONAL ADVISER

WHERE DO YOU START?

Researching universities and colleges is time well spent. Your university environment has a huge effect on your quality of life, and if you're going to be there for a few years then it makes complete sense to look hard for the place where you'll be the happiest. It's also good to think further ahead to graduation and where your university experience might lead you afterwards. There are some pointers over the page.

1 Think about the opportunities and environment you want

2 List your main requirements

3 Check university guidebooks and league tables

4 Go to higher education exhibitions and conventions

5 Look at official data

6 Read prospectuses and university websites

7 Quiz current and former students and staff

8 Make a shortlist of universities and colleges

9 Visit places on your shortlist on open days

10 Keep asking questions until you're certain

THINGS YOU MIGHT WANT TO CONSIDER

There's so much to take into account when you're wondering about where to study. You might prefer to focus on career progression, look for ways to keep debts to a minimum, or simply concentrate on finding somewhere where you feel really happy and comfortable. Try thinking about all of the following, and work out which points are likely to carry the most weight for you.

- Accommodation
- Age: traditional, 'red brick', newer college
- Amenities
- Atmosphere
- Campus or non-campus
- Cost of living
- Distance from home
- Graduate prospects
- Hobbies and interests
- Links to industry
- Mixture of students
- Non-course opportunities
- Part time work
- Reputation
- Setting
- Size, and number of undergraduates/postgraduates

- Social life
- What students say

GRADUATE PROSPECTS AND FINANCIAL ISSUES

As the cost of studying increases, and the graduate job market has become tougher in certain areas, prospective students have become increasingly focused on improving their career prospects and finding ways to fund their studies. There are many factors to consider, from post-university rates of employment to places favoured by recruiters. Minimising debt is a huge concern to many, so availability of student jobs and the local cost of living, as well as the state of tuition fees, are important things to consider too.

Graduate employment rates and wages

Chapter 1 outlined ways to find out the prospects for students of your favoured subject, and where graduates of a particular course end up working. You can also look up average employment rates and average starting salaries for entire universities. For example, if you want to know how many recent graduates are in a graduate job or further study within six months of completing their course, you can quickly find these statistics in most university guide books, such as the latest edition of *The Guardian University Guide*, or on comparison websites such as www.thecompleteuniversityguide.co.uk. Graduate salaries by university are collected by HESA in their 'Destination of Leavers' surveys, which can be found on their website in the 'Publications' section at www.hesa. ac.uk.

Graduate recruitment

Although over a third of graduate recruiters say that they don't look for people who have studied at specific universities, that still leaves some recruiters who are influenced by the name (and hopefully also the recent performance) of the institution. Many recruiters from industry and commerce target some or all the following universities: Bristol, Cambridge, Durham, Edinburgh, London School of Economics, Manchester, Nottingham, Oxford, Imperial College, Sheffield, Leeds, Birmingham, Loughborough, Bath, UMIST, Cardiff, Southampton, Brunel, Exeter and Warwick. This list varies from one employer to another, and if you have a specific career path in mind then you might want to research which universities are favoured by some of the big employers in that field. Be on the look-out for on-campus events, fairs and presentations as evidence of this targeting, and check out the contents of the latest issue of *The Times Top 100 Graduate Employers* for ideas. You can also look at graduate job market information at the official graduate careers site: www.prospects.ac.uk.

Links to industry

Some universities and colleges have strong links to local businesses, while others are better connected with national and international employers. There may be opportunities to win sponsorships, to undertake work experience, and to gain paid part-time or holiday employment. There may also be graduate schemes and mentoring. These links are sometimes found through specific departments, and sometimes via the careers service. Check prospectuses and websites to find out more.

Reputation

This can be quite tricky to gauge accurately, but when you're applying for jobs after graduation some university names can (fairly or unfairly) boost your chances of success. While some universities are undoubtedly well known and hard to get into, such as Oxford, Cambridge, Cardiff, Imperial, LSE, Edinburgh, Durham, Southampton, UCL, Warwick and so on, that doesn't mean that a particular course, teaching style or department is particularly wonderful or will suit you. Also, a reputation, negative or positive, may linger for many years even if it is no longer accurate. Reputation is perhaps something to keep in the back of your mind, but it should not be the only factor that you consider when making your choice.

University opportunities outside your course

Going to university is not only about getting good grades on your course. It's a chance to try new experiences and grow as a person, and potential employers are often just as interested in what you did at university that was non-course-related. It's a chance to make new friends, push yourself, show commitment and responsibility, and learn many transferable skills. Your university may offer a variety of extra activities, including the following.

- Presentation skills training
- Research skills courses
- Learning new languages
- IT training

- Volunteering opportunities
- Conservation schemes
- Fundraising
- National and international arts or sports competitions
- University paper, radio or TV experience

Some higher education institutions offer credits for some of these activities that can count towards the final level of your degree, so it's worth finding out whether your chosen college or university offers this credit accumulation and transfer (CAT). See www.seec-office.org.uk/credit.htm to find out more.

University career development centre/service

Many careers centres at different universities now have their own websites, which you can browse to find out more about their services and facilities. You can also drop in during university open days to see what you think.

University tuition fees

At the time of writing this book, the government had just voted to raise the cap on tuition fees to £9,000 per year from 2012. Further decisions and new legislation are likely during 2011. There will be exemptions for some students from lower-income backgrounds but others will have to pay, mainly by taking out low-interest loans. While taking out large loans might feel daunting, this might be more than offset by having good graduate prospects. Check with individual universities to find out what they intend to charge, and if you feel worried about the financial implications then talk it through with a Connexions adviser or tutor.

Cost of living

On top of your course costs, find out about the general cost of living in the area. Ask around to see what rents and bills are like, and whether you can get cheap food, drink and entertainment. Transport costs are part of the equation too, from everyday getting-around to trips back to see the parents. To track down this information, try some of the resources mentioned in Chapter 1.

Chance to earn

Part-time work is a fact of life for many students. Is there a chance to take on paid work for the university? What about nearby employers? Does your institution have a job shop on campus? How many students have part-time jobs? Does the work pay well or will you have to do loads of extra hours to make ends meet? Will any of the jobs look good on a CV? Some of this information will be found on a university's main website, or their student union website. You can also ask the university's career development centre about likely opportunities and rates of pay in the area, especially if they're responsible for running a job shop.

OTHER THINGS TO CONSIDER

Of course, there is a lot more to university life than getting a good degree, landing a graduate job, and thinking about finances. Quite a lot more, in fact. Your surroundings and everyday life are important too. Below are some more variables that might be priorities to you.

Campus or non-campus

A campus university is one where the university teaching, accommodation and leisure facilities are mostly grouped together in one place. They are often found in the outskirts of cities. Some of the more established campus universities have grown so large that they have one or more extra sites now. Non-campus (or collegiate) universities are often older and more traditional, tend to be based in a town or city, are much more spread out over different sites, and may be comprised of different colleges. Occasionally, just to be confusing, the different sites of collegiate universities are sometimes referred to as campuses.

Size

You may like to attend a smaller college or university, where you can get to know everyone. On the other hand it might make you feel like a big fish in a small pond. Or perhaps you'd prefer to go somewhere much larger where you can meet many more people, even though sometimes you might feel more anonymous or lost in the crowd. The number of people in your department and course year may be just as important as the overall size of the institution.

Age

Would you like to go somewhere that's traditional, established, and has a long history? Or would you be better off somewhere more modern, either in its buildings, its outlook or teaching methods? If a traditional university or college doesn't appeal, would you be happier at one of the further education colleges that have recently started to offer higher education courses?

Setting

There really is something for everyone here. You can find yourself studying in a big metropolitan city, an industrial heartland, a large town, a picturesque small town, a campus in the middle of the countryside, or near to mountains, hiking country, or the sea. Look areas up on maps to see how large they are, and what's nearby.

....

❛ I don't want to move away, I have too much keeping me here in terms of my friends and my family, which I wouldn't want to leave. That made the choice fairly limited. There are a few local universities, (Newcastle, Northumbria, Sunderland and a bit further afield, Durham). I chose not to apply to Durham as the business school is based in Stockton, which is quite a bit further from my house and I overall didn't really fancy it. ❜
LIZZIE JOBES, AGE 20

Distance from home

Sometimes it's good to strike out on your own, and explore a completely different environment for a few years. Or you may decide to stay closer to home to save on transport costs, be nearer to your existing social network, or keep an existing job and study a part-time degree. One of the main reasons behind the recent increase in young people remaining in the family home while studying, is the wish to save money and minimise debt. Ultimately only you can decide whether this is the best option for you or not.

Atmosphere

Is the pace of life hectic, average or laid back? Is it noisy or quiet? Is there a 'buzz' about the whole place, or just the university, or certain departments? Is it formal or informal? Is the place in good condition or run down? Are people serious, fashionable, fun-loving, friendly, competitive?

....

❛ I went to an open day at York and it was so attractive, it made me want to start studying there straight away.

Everything looked really nice, so clean and open. Most of all there was a good atmosphere. All the people I met were friendly. I applied early to give myself the best chance and right now I am waiting to hear their decision. **,**

ANONYMOUS STUDENT, AGE 17

Accommodation

Is university accommodation provided for the first year to all new students? Is it large traditional halls or smaller flats? How near is it to the buildings where you'll be studying? Do students have to share rooms, kitchens or bathrooms? Is it catered or self-catering? Are there common rooms, a bar, laundry facilities, cleaners, telephones? Can students get internet access? What are the security arrangements? How safe it is walking around at night? Is there secure parking or bicycle storage? For students who do not stay in halls, what other accommodation is available? What condition is it in, how many share one dwelling on average, where are most of the properties, and how much do they cost?

Amenities

Academic resources to consider include high quality main and departmental libraries, lecture theatres and tutorial rooms, computer labs, science and other practical labs, copying and printing resources and so on. You might also want to look at sporting facilities, such as a running track, sports pitches, subsidised university gym or swimming pool. The institution may also have a busy student union building, student health or counselling centre, a careers centre, an employment office, on-site cinema, places to eat, one or more bars, theatres, stages for bands to play, a nightclub, a bookshop, a stationery shop, etc.

Hobbies and interests

You might be hoping to continue with some of your favourite hobbies, or you might like to take up some new ones. If you're the sporty type, do you want to get a bit of exercise and boost your social life, or could you cut it in an award-winning team or national event? Being a high achiever in a particular sport can give your application form the edge with some colleges and universities. You might need a certain environment too: rock climbers and hikers might like to be near the Peak District, for example, and surfers could be drawn to Cornwall.

Or are you more likely to be interested in somewhere that has a thriving arts, music or theatre scene, whether at the university or nearby?

Social life

Depending upon your preferences, you can pick somewhere relatively quiet, somewhere with a busy social scene based on campus, or a lively city or town with a busy nightlife. If you want to be extra sociable, look for a university or college that supports several clubs and societies.

Mixture of students

If you want to encounter a variety of other cultures and maybe improve your language skills, you can try a place with a high proportion of overseas students. Or you may be a mature student who wants to study somewhere that has a high intake of people your age. Or you might just be interested in the male-female ratio (I can't imagine why!). These sorts of statistics can be found on the UCAS website, which has information on most institutions.

What other students think

To gain the best idea of the whole student experience at a particular college or university, ask a cross-section of current students and recent graduates what the place is really like. That could be relatives, neighbours, student reviewers on www.whatuni.com, or students who use online message boards such as www.yougo.co.uk, or www.thestudentroom.co.uk. You can also view the results of student surveys: for example, the results of the annual National Student Survey can be found at Unistats (www.unistats.com).

Green credentials

If you're interested in places that are environmentally friendly or sustainable, you can have a look at the People & Planet *Green League*. It's an annual independent report which contains a league table of universities' environmental performances (http://peopleandplanet.org/greenleague).

You can also read the contents of the annual Green Gown awards at www.goodcampus.org.

Extra requirements

These can be anything from childcare facilities and financial support for students with children (start with www.direct.gov.uk and university websites), to accessibility and other issues for students with disabilities (try www.skill.org.uk or their free helpline on 0800 328 5050).

RESEARCHING COLLEGES AND UNIVERSITIES

Once you've come up with a rough idea of the kind of place you'd like to attend, make a shortlist of the things that are most important to you, as well as other features you'd quite like but which aren't essential. Next, use some of the many university guides, and perhaps league tables, to find several institutions that might fit your requirements. Remember at this early stage that nothing is set in stone; be prepared to be flexible and repeat steps if necessary:

University guides

There are several university guidebooks and websites available. They are useful at this stage because they can give you quick access to summaries of lots of different institutions, so you can easily browse through to find several that interest you. Each guide has its own style and flavour, ranging from the deeply serious to the downright irreverent, and you may wish to refer to more than one to get a better combined overview:

- *The Guardian University Guide*, by Kristen Harrison and Chris Addison, contains advice on what to study, where to go, and how to get there. It includes student reports of what universities are like.
- *The Times Good University Guide* by John O'Leary is quite technical and includes a lot of statistics. It evaluates the strengths and weaknesses of each university, and provides detailed information about getting into Oxford and Cambridge.
- *The Virgin Guide to British Universities* by Piers Dudgeon contains many contributions from students themselves, and gives a good sense of the true experience of studying at a particular institution.
- *Choosing Your Degree Course & University* by Brian Heap is a comprehensive guide for anyone who is unsure about what or where to study. It discusses types of degree, career aspirations, and teaching quality.

League tables

Many newspapers publish league tables every year, each claiming to show you which institution is 'the best', or which course is 'the best'. The results often differ, as each league table is decided by weighting a range of different factors, not all of which will be a priority for you. Therefore, while they're useful for background research, you should not make any strong assumptions after reading a single table.

- *The Times* league tables are found in *The Times Good University Guide,* and are also available online at www.timesonline.co.uk (a paywall fee applies for using the website).
- *The Sunday Times* league tables are compiled in a different way, so you might like to view them too at http://extras.timesonline.co.uk/stug/universityguide.php.
- The *Guardian* league tables are compiled by giving marks out of ten for various factors, rather than presenting raw data. Find them at www.guardian.co.uk/education/universityguide.
- *The Complete University Guide* is only available online. It allows you to customise your search by selecting your own criteria, at www.thecompleteuniversityguide.co.uk.

Official statistics

So far, your search will probably have been quite general, and much of what you've heard and read will have been fairly subjective since the writers and compilers of the information each have their own ideas about what's important and what's not. Treat it all with caution until you've double checked some of the important facts about the universities you're considering.

The UCAS Institution Guide is found on their website and covers the majority of courses and institutions in the UK. It provides reliable but basic information about student numbers, accommodation, location, campuses and so on. It also displays contact details for every institution and links through to their websites so that you can continue your research, at www.ucas.com/students/choosingcourses/choosinguni/instguide.

The Department for Business, Innovation & Skills (BIS) hosts a list of all the institutions in the UK that are recognised as degree-awarding universities and university colleges, and that provide courses that lead to recognised degrees. It also names listed institutions that offer courses leading to degrees that are awarded by recognised bodies. Go to http://www.dcsf.gov.uk/recognisedukdegrees.

If you want to read about institutions and the subjects they offer in greater depth, you can try the British Council website for its Institution Search profiles. They have been written primarily for overseas students but are useful to all applicants: http://icontact.winet.com/BritishCouncil/InstitutionSearch.aspx.

University prospectuses, course-specific prospectuses and university websites usually contain most of the information you're looking for, so collect as many as you want and read them thoroughly. Contact admissions staff for more information if needed. Remember that this is a marketing exercise for them to some extent, so while they're unlikely to tell fibs, they're only going to show themselves in the most positive light. Be prepared to do some more digging before you start to narrow down those options.

❛ Keele's prospectus was the first university prospectus I ever looked at to be honest, and though I still have a bag full of 15 others, none of them really topped Keele. I like it because of the location, it's in the countryside so it won't be too much of a culture shock for me coming from a small town, but it's really easy to get into Newcastle-under-Lyme and Stoke if I'm looking for stuff to do – so it's the best of both worlds. The School of Politics, International Relations and Philosophy is also good, and does a good politics course which was an attraction for me. It also offers study abroad opportunities and because I've never been abroad I would love to do this. Not just for a holiday (honest!) but because it adds something extra to my degree and I would like to experience a different culture. ❜

SOPHIE W, AGE 18, DEBEN HIGH SCHOOL (SUFFOLK)

Talking to people

Take every chance you can to discuss possible colleges or universities with current and former students, or friends and relatives who have lived in those areas. Higher education advisers or careers counsellors may be able to give you ideas or suggest some recommended reading too. Keep in mind that some people might be a bit biased or their information may be out of date. Once you've done a little more research you can email or phone university staff with any queries you might have – don't be scared to ask questions, even if they seem a bit silly at the time.

Higher education conventions and exhibitions

UCAS runs over 50 conventions and subject-specific exhibitions around the UK each year. Some are large central events for anyone who's interested in higher education, and others are more local. Most conventions are not subject-specific and attract exhibitors from all of the institutions that use UCAS to handle their applications. Some have a narrower range of subjects, and may be devoted to performing arts, design, or the health professions. Conventions and exhibitions are an ideal opportunity to speak in depth with staff from a range of institutions all on the same day. They also attract other organisations such as student travel firms, professional bodies, student support services, Connexions staff and gap year organisations. Entry is free, and you can turn up without booking.

You will get the most out of a convention or fair if you've already done some preliminary research into what and where you'd like to study. This should give you a 'hit list' of stands and staff to target, preferably with a pleasant smile and a few questions. Look at the programme before you arrive to see who's going to be there, and check for the timing of any interesting presentations or seminars. Pick up a floor plan of exhibitors at the front door as you arrive, which will allow you to decide on the quickest route to take to get around all your favourites. Then if you have time left over afterwards you can browse around the convention hall and find out more about other institutions that you might not already have considered.

Ask the advisers anything you like, such as: entry requirements, selection procedures, course structure and assessment, self-directed learning, costs, sponsorship opportunities, facilities and support, general questions about the institution, graduate prospects, contact details, and where to go for more information. Pick up as many relevant leaflets and prospectuses as you can. You may also want to attend seminars on the day about filling in application forms, writing personal statements, or taking gap years.

Find out more at www.ucas.com/events and www.ucasevents.com/conventions. There's also a pre-convention planner to help you prepare at www.ucas.com/events/howtoprepare/actionplan.

Open days

Visiting a higher education institution allows you to see what it's like for yourself and make your own mind up. Universities hold departmental open days, open days for their individual colleges, and university-wide open days. Try to visit as many as your time and finances allow, although you will have to balance the number of visits out against the disruption to your studies or employment.

Full listings of all British university open days can be found here: www.opendays.com/calendar, and you can also check university websites. As dates may be announced late or subject to change, you should also contact institutions nearer the time you plan to visit to ensure that they will be proceeding as planned.

To get the very best out of the day, write a checklist of whatever's important to you. Take a notebook along with you and write down what you find out as a reminder for when you get home. Observe your surroundings, reflect on your feelings, and ask as many questions as you need to. Talk to students, and academic and support staff.

A sample checklist might be as follows:

Course
- [ ] How interesting is the course?
- [ ] Any bits that look boring?
- [ ] Can I do well here?
- [ ] Entry requirements
- [ ] What current students say
- [ ] Careers this course could lead to
- [ ] Recognised by professional bodies?

- [ ] What's the department like?
- [ ] Who are the lecturers?
- [ ] How many students in each year?
- [ ] Course structure and flexibility
- [ ] Work experience or industrial placements
- [ ] Links with employers
- [ ] Teaching style

- ☐ Amount of independent study
- ☐ Facilities such as labs, equipment, lecture halls, etc.
- ☐ Key or transferable skills
- ☐ Chance to study abroad?

University

- ☐ What's the general atmosphere like?
- ☐ Type and size of campus
- ☐ Condition of buildings
- ☐ Where is my department?
- ☐ Does the campus feel friendly, safe?
- ☐ Is there anywhere to eat and drink?
- ☐ Access for disabled students
- ☐ What's the nearby town or city like?
- ☐ Extra-curricular learning opportunities
- ☐ Do I feel relaxed and at home here?

Transport

- ☐ Where are the transport links?
- ☐ How much does it cost?
- ☐ Will there be a lot of travel between campuses?
- ☐ Parking space, bike racks?

Support

- ☐ Student health services
- ☐ Employment centre
- ☐ Careers centre
- ☐ Student Union

- ☐ Welfare officers
- ☐ Disability officers
- ☐ Financial advisers

Facilities

- ☐ Library
- ☐ Lecture theatres and seminar rooms
- ☐ Computer labs
- ☐ Practical rooms
- ☐ Bars and clubs
- ☐ Sports fields, sports centres
- ☐ Launderette
- ☐ Shops

Accommodation

- ☐ How near to campus?
- ☐ Catered or self-catering?
- ☐ Safe area, security measures?
- ☐ Condition of buildings (inside and out)?
- ☐ How many sharing?
- ☐ How often are bills paid?
- ☐ What do students need to bring?
- ☐ What facilities are there?

Costs/financial

- ☐ Tuition fees
- ☐ Other fees
- ☐ Course equipment
- ☐ Field trips
- ☐ Cost of living
- ☐ Funding
- ☐ Sponsorship
- ☐ Bursaries

- ☐ Deposits
- ☐ Part time jobs

Graduate prospects

- ☐ Percentage of graduates employed
- ☐ Drop out rates
- ☐ Type of work graduates end up in
- ☐ Employers who visit the department/uni
- ☐ Further study options

- ☐ What students think of the careers centre
- ☐ Facilities at the careers centre

Social

- ☐ Clubs and societies
- ☐ Places to meet friends
- ☐ Practice rooms
- ☐ Nearby nightlife
- ☐ Cultural: theatre, art, music, cinema

It's up to you what questions you decide to ask, but as you can see, investigating a college or university can be quite a complex process.

....

❜ I've had identical offers from LSE and UCL and I don't know which to pick. The course structures are similar and they both have the same high reputation, but I'm completely stuck. I want somewhere with a good social life, if it comes down to it. I do know I want to move to London. Probably going to have to visit them both again to make my mind up, and do some more research. ❜

CHARLES, AGE 17

Pre-university taster courses

Another way of finding out what a university or college is really like is to participate in a 'taster' course there. These vary in length, from a one day course to a longer summer school lasting a few weeks, and can be residential or non-residential. They range from sixth-form workshops to master-classes, study days and activity weeks. Subjects vary but are often scientific or technical. They may be free or run by commercial companies that charge fees

It's an ideal way to show genuine interest in a course or subject, and it looks good on an application form. Taster courses can also give you the inside view of what a department's really like. To find out more, try the latest edition of *Open Days* (published by UCAS), or apply directly to institutions that you're interested in.

STUDYING OUTSIDE THE UK

An increasing number of UK students are deciding to study for their degrees outside of the UK. A full guide to this mode of study is outside the scope of this book, but here are some useful starting points.

Republic of Ireland

The Central Applications Office (CAO) handles all applications to universities in the Republic of Ireland. Their website contains an online application form, details of all courses and institutions, an application handbook, and details of university open days.

Central Applications Office
Tower House
Eglinton Street
Galway
Ireland
Tel: 00 353 (0)91 509800
Fax: 00 353 (0)91 562344
Web: www.cao.ie/index.php

UKCISA

The UK Council for International Student Affairs (UKCISA) suggest that if you want to study for a whole degree abroad, you will normally need to start researching possibilities 12–18 months in advance to allow sufficient time for making an application, completing any tests (including language tests) required, obtaining visas and finding funding.

UKCISA
9–17 St Albans Place
London N1 0NX
Advice Line: 020 7107 9922

For help and advice, visit their web pages for UK students studying abroad: www.ukcisa.org.uk/student/ukstudent/index.php.

The British Council

This organisation is the UK's international educational opportunities and cultural relations body. It runs various educational schemes and awards, and provide a wide range of information about studying abroad.

British Council Information Centre
Bridgewater House
58 Whitworth Street
Manchester M1 6BB
Tel: 0161 957 7755
Web: www.britishcouncil.org

Braintrack University Index

Braintrack (www.braintrack.com) is the world's oldest and most complete university directory, with over 8,300 links to higher education institutions in 194 countries. You can find universities by browsing countries or by advanced search.

SUMMARY: TEN TIPS FOR CHOOSING A UNIVERSITY

1. There's no 'best' university. There's only the best combination of course, subject, department, institution, prospects and overall environment *for you*.

2. See the big picture. Don't be too easily swayed by one single book, website, or person's opinion. Do plenty of reading and asking around to get a balanced overview.

3. The future is now. While graduate prospects are important, there are many other things to consider too. You will be at university for a few years before you graduate, so make sure you choose an environment in which you will feel comfortable and happy.

4. Make a shortlist. Once you have an overview, start researching a few attractive institutions in much greater detail. You can begin to narrow your choices down from there.

5. Check official information. Make sure you're applying to a proper course at a recognised or listed institution. Especially important if you're applying for an unusual or novel course, or considering a college you've never encountered before.

6. Attend higher education conferences. Get quality information from representatives from several institutions all under the same roof, and attend useful presentations.

7. Collect prospectuses and course guides. They will help you to decide where to apply to, and give advice on how to write your applications and perform well at interviews. Just remember that they won't tell you about the downside of anything.

8. Attend open days. There's no substitute for visiting in person and making your own mind up. Make a checklist before you arrive, and take notes throughout the day.

9. Keep asking questions. Speak to careers advisers if you get stuck, and contact university admissions offices if information is unclear or incomplete.

10. Consider a taster course. See how a department functions on an everyday level, and have something good to add to an application form. Attending some summer schools can also lead to being made offers with lower entry requirements.

CHAPTER FOUR

THE APPLICATION

I f you've completely made your mind up about courses you want to apply to, and places you'd like to study, you can begin to prepare your application. The majority of applications are made through UCAS's standard online application process, but there are differences in timing and form-filling if you're applying for medicine, dentistry, veterinary medicine and science, some art and design courses, and any undergraduate courses at Oxford or Cambridge.

Some teacher training and music courses are applied for through other bodies and, under certain circumstances, applications are also made directly to colleges and universities themselves, such as applications to the Open University. These will be mentioned later, but let's start by concentrating upon the main UCAS route.

The quicker you can get your application started, the better, because that way you don't end up rushing and badly stressed before the deadline. It's pretty easy to do, I was expecting it to be so much more complicated. So long as you get someone to talk you through it first it's a stress-free process. Plus you can have it checked a few times at college before you send it off, which is good. Our staff could not have been more helpful.

ANONYMOUS STUDENT

AN OVERVIEW OF THE STANDARD UCAS APPLICATION PROCESS

Most applications for UK degree courses are made through a standard process run by UCAS. If everything goes well, the most common route is that you apply online via UCAS, are made an offer by your favourite university, you accept this as a firm offer (plus one insurance place), you get your grades, and you confirm your place. However, if things don't go according to this simple plan, you also have the opportunity to apply through the UCAS Extra, Adjustment and Clearing processes. This process is outlined in the diagram on p. 63.

The process is slightly different if you are applying via UCAS for dentistry, medicine, veterinary medicine and science, and some art and design courses, or if you're hoping to enter Oxford or Cambridge. A few courses are also applied for outside of the UCAS system. These variations will all be mentioned later in this chapter. For more information about UCAS Extra, please turn to Chapter 7: Offers, rejections and UCAS Extra, later in this book, which is followed by Chapter 8: Clearing and Adjustment.

APPLICATION DEADLINES

Once you've chosen your ideal courses it's absolutely essential that you carefully check the application deadlines for each one, and if you're not certain then check directly with the individual universities themselves. The typical application year runs according to the table on page 64.

Wherever possible, don't leave it until the last second to apply for courses in case you miss the deadlines. Vacancies on the most popular courses fill up quickly, and admissions tutors can start offering places as soon as they receive your application. However, Darren Barker from UCAS says: 'Students don't have to rush to get their application in as long as they make the deadline. Admissions staff in universities and colleges use a wealth of experience built up from previous years when setting their entry standards and criteria, so can promise to consider equally all applications which are received on time.'

☑ **TIP**

The deadlines in the table on p. 64 are for completed applications being sent to UCAS. If you are applying through your school or college then you may have to prepare your application before this, in order to get help from staff and referees. Allow extra time for this.

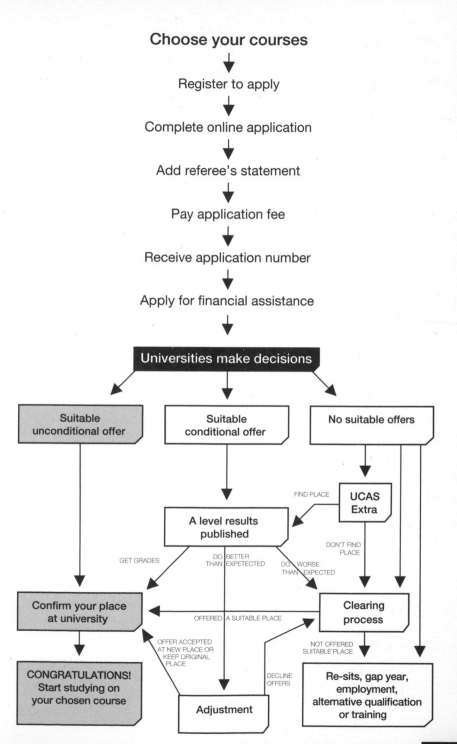

Choose your courses

Register to apply

Complete online application

Add referee's statement

Pay application fee

Receive application number

Apply for financial assistance

Universities make decisions

Suitable unconditional offer

Suitable conditional offer

No suitable offers

UCAS Extra

FIND PLACE

A level results published

DON'T FIND PLACE

GET GRADES

DO BETTER THAN EXPETECTED

DO WORSE THAN EXPECTED

Confirm your place at university

OFFERED A SUITABLE PLACE

Clearing process

CONGRATULATIONS! Start studying on your chosen course

OFFER ACCEPTED AT NEW PLACE OR KEEP ORIGINAL PLACE

NOT OFFERED SUITABLE PLACE

DECLINE OFFERS

Adjustment

Re-sits, gap year, employment, alternative qualification or training

Table 1 Application deadline timetable

Start of September	Applications open for courses commencing the following September/October
Mid-October	Deadline for UCAS applications for medicine, dentistry, veterinary medicine and veterinary science
Mid-October	Deadline for UCAS applications for Oxford and Cambridge
Mid-January	Deadline for most UCAS course applications (consideration not guaranteed after this date). This includes applications from overseas students too.
End of February	First date that some students become eligible to apply for courses using the UCAS Extra process (see Chapter 7)
3rd week of March	Deadline for application for certain art and design courses. Check individual course information for details of deadlines.
End of June	Last chance for UK, European Union and international students to apply for full-time courses through UCAS (consideration not guaranteed)
Start of July	Deadline for applying for courses via Extra, if eligible.

STANDARD UCAS APPLICATIONS

Almost all UCAS applications are now made online. The UCAS Apply system is a secure, web-based application system, which is available 24 hours a day. You fill in the application online when it suits you, and it does not need to be completed all at once – so you are able to practise and take your time (you have the option to store and edit your details in Apply without submitting them). You can fill in the online form at any computer with internet access, and as soon as you're happy and decide to submit it, the information goes immediately to UCAS, and then it's forwarded to your chosen universities and colleges.

Darren Barker from UCAS points out that: 'All the information about making a UCAS application is available on www.ucas.com and if students have signed up to the UCAS Card scheme, they will receive information in the form of e-bulletins and other help guiding them through the procedure. Tutors and advisers should also be well versed in the UCAS application process.' If you're no longer in education then you can apply as an independent applicant, and there will be slight differences in the way you fill the form in, which will be mentioned as we go along.

Here's the running order for completing the standard UCAS online application.

1 Register online at www.ucas.com

2 Log in to Apply

3 Check/fill in your personal details

4 Complete the additional information section (UK entrants only)

5 Fill in your choices

6 Fill in education section

7 Complete employment section

8 Cut and paste in Personal Statement

9 Reference is added (by you or referee)

10 Final editing (if referee says it's needed)

11 Agree to the declaration

12 Form is submitted (by you or referee)

13 Pay UCAS

14 UCAS forwards applications to institutions

15 Use the online 'Track' system to follow progress

IMPORTANT! MAKE SURE YOU DON'T LOSE . . .

- Your school or college 'buzzword' (if there is one)
- The email address you gave to UCAS
- Your Track username/ID number
- The Track password you've chosen
- Your UCAS application number

❝ I tried to log into my UCAS Track with a completely incorrect password too many times. It then told me that my account had been suspended and I got worried in case that meant my applications would not be sent off to my unis. But don't worry, it only means that you cannot log onto it for the next 24–48 hours. I can guarantee you that it will unlock itself, and if not you can call UCAS for help. ❞

SAM, AGE 18

FILLING IN THE UCAS APPLICATION FORM

The Apply system is fairly simple to use, with help text available throughout to assist you to complete each section. There is also detailed advice on the UCAS website (www.ucas.com), and if you still can't find what you're looking for, you can contact the UCAS Customer Service Unit on 0871 468 0468 to speak to an adviser (or 0044 871 468 0468 if calling from outside the UK). If you're at school or college, your tutors should also be able to explain things and troubleshoot many problems.

Technical problems

The online system is designed for viewing using a browser such as Internet Explorer version 5 and above, and other browsers such as Mozilla Firefox version 2.0 and above. Most users have no technical problems at all, but there are two online guides to help you cope with the occasional glitch: www.ucas.com/advisers/online/techissues/settings **and** www.ucas.com/advisers/online/techissues/knownissues.

ONLINE CENTRES

If you don't have access to a personal computer with an internet connection, and you're fighting for computer time at college or school, there is an alternative option. Over 900 online centres are participating in a scheme with UCAS and will allow you to use their computers for free. They will not be able to offer you any support or advice specific to the application, but you will be able to view the UCAS website, set up an account, and use Apply and Track. See www.ukonlinecentres.com for more information and to find your nearest centre.

'I found getting into Apply was all fine. It didn't take me too much time at all to complete the form. It was getting it through my school system that took the longest time! I didn't use a leaflet, nor did I need to – it was all very obvious. I didn't really have any problems at all, except that it took a bit of time to find all the music qualifications and getting the orders right for my exams. Oh, it WAS a little confusing as to how I entered my AS levels and A levels, whether we had to enter both or not etc . . . The only thing I could be picky about is that the form kept coming back to me with "errors" from my form tutor, although neither of us could find them. That was a bit annoying but it got sorted out. Apart from that it made total sense, was not difficult at all, and for the most part it was reliable! The odd server downtime interrupted my application and meant I lost any unsaved info, but otherwise it was comprehensive and easy to use. '
ALEX CLAYTON, OSSETT SIXTH FORM, AGE 18

Getting started: registration

You need to register first before you can use Apply. Even at this early stage, take great care over your spelling and use of upper and lower case letters.

University staff will be reading some of what you type in here, so make it look like a professional document from the start, rather than a text message to your best mate.

Darren Barker says: 'If you're registering through your school, college or careers organisation, you need their "buzzword", which will be given to you by your tutor or careers adviser. When you enter this buzzword during the registration process, it links your application to your school so that your tutor can write your reference.' Buzzwords, like all Apply passwords, are case sensitive so type with care. Don't forget to use the buzzword, as without it your tutor or year head won't be able to provide you with a reference. If you do forget it, you'll have to ask your college or school to contact UCAS so that they can change your application over to the right system. You don't need a buzzword if you're applying independently.

To register, go to www.ucas.com and click on 'Apply', then click on 'Register/ Log in to Apply', and read the online instructions.

If you're applying via your school or college, click on the school or college, and then type the buzzword into the box and click 'Next'. You will be taken to a screen saying you are at a particular school or college, and if it's correct, click 'Yes' to be taken to a drop down list to select your tutor. Then click 'Next' to continue to the contact details stage.

If you're applying independently, skip the part where you click on a school or college, and you will then be asked a few questions to confirm your eligibility before you can go ahead with your application.

You will arrive at a screen where you fill in your name, gender and date of birth – make sure that the 'UK' button is selected if you're applying from the UK. Then type in your postcode and full address, telephone numbers and email address, and click 'Next'. Use an email address that you check regularly and won't forget the password for, and don't pick one that reads anything like vodkaredbull@ wasted.net or iM2Sexxi@facebookedyamum.com. The next screen will ask you to check the details you've entered so far. Go back and edit even the tiniest mistake. Once you're happy, click on 'Next'.

You will then be given your unique Apply username, and asked to choose a password. Write both of them down and keep them somewhere very safe. Then you will be asked to create four security questions that only you know the answers to, just in case you need to call UCAS for help, so that they can prove your identity. You can now decide whether to go straight on and continue with the rest of the application, or come back later.

If you do decide to come back to the application after taking a break, go to www.ucas.com and click on 'Apply', then 'Student login', and type in your registration username and password. If you get it wrong too many times you will get locked out of the system. If you're confused at any point, you can use the 'How to use Apply' help information.

Click on any section title to open it (you can complete them in any order) and add to it. You can save what you've done so far if you need to take a break at any time. Once you're happy that a section has been totally completed, click the 'Section finished' button and go on to the next one.

☑ TIP

Your email address must be verified before you can proceed with the application process. Look out for a verification email from UCAS that allows you to confirm your email address. Once this is done, UCAS will be able to send you reminders and updates, and process your application.

Personal

Your name, title, home address, phone numbers, date of birth, gender and emails will be on this part of the form already – check they're all correct. You will then be asked to supply your country of birth, your nationality, your residential status, and information about your financial arrangements. Take care when entering student support codes and other financial data, as one common mistake is saying you're privately funded when you aren't (being completely privately funded is relatively uncommon, and is not about having a high parental income or applying for student loans).

Next, you'll be asked about special needs: this includes dyslexia, disabilities and chronic health conditions such as diabetes and epilepsy. You will also be asked whether you have any criminal convictions. Do NOT tick this box if, like most students, you have no criminal convictions against you.

You will also be given a non-compulsory option to give nominated access. This is where you nominate someone, such as a parent/guardian or adviser/mentor, who can discuss your application with UCAS and the universities if you're unavailable. If you decide to use this option, enter their name and relationship to you.

Additional information

This is for UK applicants only, and you can expect to be asked about the following.

- **Ethnic origin and national identity.** This is not passed on to universities until after places have been offered. The questions are compulsory, and if you don't want to answer then you must select the 'I prefer not to say' option.
- **Activities in preparation for higher education.** You can enter up to two courses here if you like, such as summer schools, Saturday university, campus days, summer academies, taster courses and booster courses.
- **Care and parental education.** Optional questions.
- **Parental occupation.** This question is compulsory, but you can select the 'I prefer not to say' option. Again, this is not passed on to your chosen universities during the application and selection process.

Choices

Normally you have up to five choices, but you don't have to use them all and can pick only one if you like. Applying for more than one course at the same university counts as more than one choice.

None of the universities you apply to will be told about which other institutions you've applied to, so don't worry that this will somehow count against you. However, if you apply for two or more different courses at the same university or college, that institution will know that you have applied for more than one place with them.

There are special considerations if you're applying for medicine/dentistry/ veterinary medicine/veterinary science (see page 77 of this chapter) or courses at either the University of Oxford or the University of Cambridge (see page 77).

You may need to add in some extra course-specific information for certain courses. Check the UCAS website for every course you choose to see whether there's anything in the 'Details required to fill in your UCAS form' section. There could be admissions tests, proof of Hepatitis B immunisation, or agreement to submit to a criminal records check, depending upon the subject you wish to study. You may also be asked to give course codes, for example, for certain language courses.

☑ TIP

If you don't use up all your five choices to start with, you can add more later if you change your mind – so long as you do it before the relevant UCAS or course deadline.

There will also be some more boxes to fill in or leave blank for each separate course:

- one to tick if you wish to live in your present home while you are at university
- 'Defer entry' (if you're applying now, but planning to take a year off before starting your studies, you need to remind the college or university of your intentions)
- 'Point of entry' (leave blank unless you want to apply for entry into the second year at a university in Scotland).

Be certain that you have done these correctly for every single course before you mark the section as complete.

At the end of this section, applicants who are not still at school will be asked about previous applications through UCAS.

PLANNING A DEFERRAL?

The usual application deadlines for the current year will still apply to you, and if you accept a place for the following year you cannot then reapply for other places during the following year unless you withdraw your original application. If you are going to defer, you must fill in the correct box on the online application to make it official.

Applying a year ahead is by far the easiest thing to do if you're still at school or college and planning a gap year. You'll be on site and able to communicate with tutors and referees more easily, and there should be plenty of help during the application process if you get stuck. If you leave it until the following academic year you might not get this level of support, and it can be hard to make arrangements if you're working or travelling overseas. There's more about gap years and deferral in Chapter 1 of this book.

Education

First you need to fill in the places where you have studied. If you haven't finished school yet, fill in the date you started, and leave the 'Date of leaving' box blank. Then click on the 'Add qualification' link and enter all your qualifications by clicking on the correct category (GCSE/GCE, AS and A level, Other etc.), and making sure you enter the exact title of the subject, the date taken (if completed), and the right examination board. If you can't find your qualification in the list that's offered, click 'O' in the A–Z list and select the relevant 'Other' option. If Entry Profiles in Course Search for your course choices ask for specific units or module results then you will be able to add these in here too.

The summary screen will list your qualifications. If you haven't taken the exams yet, they will be highlighted as 'Pending'. Universities base their offers upon your qualifications, so make sure they're correct and remember, they can check up on them. You will also be asked to enter your highest level of qualification so far – remember that this does not include the degree course that you're applying to.

If you get stuck while entering your education details, there's a handy UCAS guide at www.ucas.com/students/applying/howtoapply/education/quals.

Employment

This section is for any paid work you have done, including up to five full time, part time and holiday jobs. Remember to put the name of the company down, and not the name of your manager. Don't include volunteer work or unpaid work experience in this section. If you have a long employment history you can also send your full work history directly to the colleges and universities you're applying to after you've filled in everything else on the form. If you haven't had a job before, don't worry. Just leave the section blank, then mark it as 'Complete' and carry on with the rest of the application.

Personal statement

The personal statement is usually prepared in a separate word processing document, then cut and pasted into the online Apply form.

This section is the only part of the form where applicants get to write anything substantial in their own words. It's an excellent opportunity to explain why your chosen course interests you and the reasons you think you'd make a good candidate. On courses where there's intense competition for spaces, this can make or break your application. In fact, it's so important to get it right that the whole of Chapter 5 of this guide is devoted to it – please flip through to find out more.

The personal statement can strongly influence whether you're made an offer or not. At universities and colleges that hold interviews, many interview questions concentrate on aspects of the personal statement, so it's essential to be both interesting and honest in your writing.

The reference

A full written reference is required, preferably from someone in an official capacity who knows you well. It is not permitted to gain references from friends, relatives or partners.

Darren Barker from UCAS runs us through the responsibilities of applicants and referees: 'If an applicant is at school or college, or has recently left, then they should get the head teacher, principal or an appropriate teacher to write the reference. Once an applicant has completed their online application, they then send it to their referee, who will then check through it and write their reference. The referee will then send it to UCAS. Applicants applying through a school or college don't have access to the reference.

'If an applicant is applying as an individual, they should ask a responsible person who knows them well enough to provide their reference. This could be an employer, training officer, careers adviser, a teacher on a recent relevant further education course, or a senior colleague in employment or voluntary work. It is the applicant's responsibility to obtain the reference and add it to their online application before sending the application to UCAS.' You will need to cut and paste their reference into the form.

If you're applying through your school, college or centre, you need to complete your whole application and pay UCAS (if applicable) before sending the application off to the referee. See page 75 for more about payment.

☑ TIP

Remember to keep your referee informed of your progress to give them plenty of time to prepare their reference.

Sending off the application

Once you have completed all the sections of the form that you need to, check and edit it until you're happy, then print out some paper copies of the form to keep.

As mentioned above, school or college applicants need to send the application to their referee, who might come back to them for some more editing, and who will then forward it to UCAS. You will be asked to agree to a declaration. Read it carefully before ticking the box and clicking 'I agree'.

Independent applicants forward the form to UCAS themselves by agreeing to the declaration, then moving on to arrange payment.

Payment

If you're applying through your school, college or centre, your organisation will let you know how and when they want you to pay. It will be either by credit or debit card online via the Apply system, or by paying the school or other registered centre which will then pay UCAS on your behalf. If applying as an individual, you will need to make your payment via the Apply system using a credit or debit card. The card need not be in your own name, but you will require the consent of the cardholder. If you're applying for more than one course, it costs £21 to use the Apply service. If you only apply to one course at one university or college, you pay £11.

Congratulations! Your application is now on its way. Good luck.

Once you have completed your application and sent it, you will get a message saying that the application has been sent to UCAS (or it will be sent to your referee if you're applying through a school, college or other organisation). Once the application has been processed, you will be sent a welcome letter in the post, also known as an AS2. If the details it contains are incorrect, or it hasn't arrived within 14 days of you completing the application, contact the UCAS Customer Service Unit (0871 468 0 468).

USING TRACK TO MONITOR YOUR PROGRESS

UCAS's welcome letter will include a personal ID number and explain how to use the online Track function. You will be able to follow the progress of your application, and update your address details, if they've changed, using Track. For all options you will need to know your original username and password that you used with Apply.

As each university or college decides upon your application, UCAS updates the details on Track. You can check online regularly, or sign up to be alerted by email or text message when these changes are made. The decisions are listed on the website, but will not be detailed in emails or texts to protect your privacy.

Each university has its own process for dealing with admissions. You may be asked to write essays or attend interviews or test sessions (see Chapter 6), or you may simply receive offers or rejections (see Chapter 7). Universities should aim to send all decisions to applicants by the end of March, so long as the application was received before the middle of January. In practice, some universities do not reply until the start of the second week of May, and if they're later than this with their reply it becomes a rejection by default.

> **❝** There is this stupid joke among me and my friends that we're all addicted to Track. I have been known to check it up to five times a day and I don't think I'll be able to relax until all my five choices have replied to me. I know if anything changes they will send me an email, I know it's updated automatically more than once an hour, but I just can't seem to help myself! **❞**
>
> **PAUL GOLDBERG, AGE 17**

☑ TIP

Apply for financial help – student grants, student loans and bursaries – as soon as you've made your applications. You don't need to wait for the offer of a course.

CHANGING YOUR UCAS APPLICATION

If your personal details change, such as your home address, phone number or email address, you should let UCAS know immediately. This can be done on Track or by contacting Customer Services (0871 468 0 468).

Sometimes applicants have a change of heart about their choice of one or more of their universities or colleges. If that happens to you, you can change your university or college choices on Track, but only if you do so within 14 days of receiving your welcome letter. After 14 days you cannot normally change them, unless there are special circumstances and your referee writes to UCAS to explain them.

If you're happy with your choice of institution, but have changed your mind about your course, deferral, or the point of entry, you must contact the institution directly.

They will then inform UCAS of their decision and the results will be posted on Track.

UCAS strongly recommends that you ask somebody to check through your application before it is submitted to make sure that there are no errors within the form. If an error is found after submitting a form there are ways in which they can be rectified, especially if you act quickly. You should contact UCAS on 0871 468 0468 if you find yourself in such a situation, and UCAS will help you to follow the correct procedure.

For information about withdrawing your UCAS application, please refer to Chapter 7 of this guide. This is not a decision to be taken lightly; it's not the same as declining all your offers and it means you cannot enter Clearing or other services.

MEDICINE, DENTISTRY, VETERINARY MEDICINE, VETERINARY SCIENCE

You can apply to these courses using the standard UCAS service, with one exception. Rather than the standard maximum of five choices, if you apply for one of the above subjects you can only make up to four choices within that specific subject. The remaining space (or spaces) on your application can be used as an insurance choice and can be for any subject you want. Remember that your personal statement will be sent to your insurance choice too. Note the early closing date of mid-October for applications.

To accompany your application you may be asked to provide the results of entry tests by a set date (see Chapter 6 for details), and/or send proof that you have been vaccinated against the Hepatitis B virus.

APPLYING FOR OXFORD OR CAMBRIDGE

You can only apply to one course at either Oxford University or the University of Cambridge, and you can't apply to both institutions at the same time (unless you already have a degree). This leaves you with up to four choices for courses at other universities. The mid-October UCAS application deadline also applies, and you should check individual course pages to see whether you need to sit tests or provide other information.

If you're applying to Cambridge, in addition to your UCAS application you'll also have to fill in their Supplementary Application Questionnaire. Overseas students must fill in a Cambridge Overseas Application Form (COAF) too. You can submit your application to a specific College, or make an open application. For more information, see www.cam.ac.uk/admissions/undergraduate/apply.

ART AND DESIGN APPLICATIONS

Some art and design courses have an application date of the 24th of March, instead of the usual mid-January deadline. These course dates are sometimes subject to change, and it's important to check them regularly. UCAS update their list every weekday, and you can find it here: www.ucas.ac.uk/documents/ucasguides/artdes24mar.pdf

You have a standard five choices for art and design courses, and can have a mixture of courses with mid-January or 24th of March deadlines. Just be careful not to get the application dates mixed up, and check with teachers and referees about internal school or college deadlines for preparation of references, and possibly also portfolios.

NON-UCAS APPLICATIONS

While almost all undergraduate courses in the UK are now applied for via UCAS, there are a few exceptions, including music schools and some forms of teacher training.

CUKAS

The Conservatories UK Admissions Service (CUKAS) handles applications to practice-based music courses at the following UK conservatoires.

- Birmingham Conservatoire
- Leeds College of Music
- Royal College of Music
- Royal Northern College of Music
- Royal Scottish Academy of Music and Drama
- Royal Welsh College of Music and Drama
- Trinity Laban College of Music

The applications are made via a service supported by UCAS, so they are uploaded using Apply and followed using Track. Applications open in early July for admission the following year, and should ideally be submitted by the start of October for guaranteed consideration. Auditions may begin as early as mid-October. For more details on dates for applying, auditions, decisions and replying, phone CUCAS on 0871 468 0470 or see their website: www.cukas. ac.uk/students/applying.

Teacher training

You need a degree and qualified teacher status (QTS) to become a teacher. Anyone wanting to teach in England and Wales must complete initial teacher training (ITT). There are several routes into teacher training, including some applications made through UCAS. If you're unsure about the best route for you to take, call the Teaching Information Line on 0845 6000 991.

For applications for entry to Professional or Postgraduate Certificate in Education (PGCE) and Professional Graduate Diploma in Education (PGDE) courses, you need to use the Graduate Teacher Training Registry (GTTR). GTTR act on behalf of Initial Teacher Training (ITT) providers, which offer teacher training in England and Wales, and most Scottish Higher Education Institutions. GTTR applications are made online via their website, and followed using Track. For more information contact their Customer Service Unit on 0871 468 0469 from within the UK, or +44 871 468 0 469 if you are calling from outside the UK, or look up details on their website: www.gttr.ac.uk/students/howtoapply.

APPLYING FOR PART-TIME AND FLEXIBLE LEARNING

If you have decided to start part-time or flexible learning, rather than a full-time undergraduate course, you should apply directly to the institution. These details can be found on the Hotcourses website, on the www.direct. gov.uk course database powered by Learndirect, and in the prospectuses of individual higher education providers. For the Open University, you can register online (www.open.ac.uk) or by phone (0845 300 60 90).

SUMMARY:
TOP TIPS FOR APPLICATIONS

1. Keep it professional. Remember that the applications tutors will be able to see everything you've typed in, so use correct grammar, not text-speak, and put capital letters in the right places. Avoid using potentially offensive email addresses too.

2. Double check deadlines. Always check your course information for specific deadlines and other requirements. Allow plenty of time to apply so that you can get your personal statement looking perfect and the rest of your application form properly filled in with all the right information.

3. Respect the ref. You also need to give your referee enough time to write a proper personal reference for you. Keep them informed of your progress and let them know when you'll be needing their input. Be prepared to politely and persistently chase them up if necessary.

4. Don't rush it. You can save whatever you're working on in Apply and come back to it whenever you feel like it. There's no need to feel pressured into rushing the whole thing through all in one go.

5. Check for extra codes. If you apply to certain courses, especially languages, they may have additional codes to enter into the system to complete the application. Check on the UCAS website for all the details for each course you're applying to.

6. The personal statement's different. It's the only part of the form where you can put things into your own words and stand out from the crowd. Take your time over it, and do all the drafting using a word processing program first.

7. Slightly different. Note that UCAS applications for medicine, dentistry, veterinary medicine and science, Oxford and Cambridge, and a few art and design courses have variations in the way you apply. This may include extra forms, tests, and non-standard deadlines.

8. You're not alone. If you get stuck or make a big mistake in Apply, then try the UCAS website help and troubleshooting pages, and their customer service line. You may also get help from school or college tutors and careers advisers.

9. Keep Track of it all. Log into the UCAS online Track function regularly to follow your progress and to reply to requests and offers.

10. Slightly different again. Although almost all applications for undergraduate courses in the UK are made via UCAS, conservatories, some teaching courses and part time courses are applied to by different routes – check with each institution you're considering to find out how and when to apply.

CHAPTER FIVE
ADVICE FOR THE UCAS PERSONAL STATEMENT

Competition has dramatically increased for places on many university courses and your personal statement can make or break your applications, so it's worth making the effort to create one that's as well written and informative as possible. If you take the time to research and prepare properly, you'll end up with a document that helps you stand out from the other applicants, explains why you're suitable for your chosen course, and shows how motivated and committed you are.

A good personal statement will:

- Show you off in a good light and help you stand out from the crowd
- Explain why you're interested in a certain course
- Demonstrate commitment and enthusiasm
- Persuade admissions staff that you're suited to the course
- Give good examples of interests, skills and achievements
- Be well written and have a logical structure
- Contain no factual, spelling or grammatical mistakes.

> ☑ **TIP**
>
> You only get to write one personal statement, but it usually goes off to several different universities or colleges. Try not to name specific universities in your statement, or mention other things that are suitable for one course but not others you've applied to.

It's often the first time that students have been asked to write about themselves in this way, so naturally it might feel a little difficult getting started. However, it's also your chance to review the decisions that you've made so far, to reflect upon what's really important to you, and consider your strengths and weaknesses.

Here's a step-by-step guide on how to get the most out of the personal statement.

1	Think about what admissions tutors are looking for
2	Research your courses properly
3	Make lots of notes before you start writing
4	Write a careful first draft
5	Re-write it several times
6	Double check everything
7	Involve school or college staff or referees where appropriate
8	Follow UCAS's uploading instructions
9	Refer back to statement for interviews, Clearing, UCAS Extra, etc.

Beth Hayes, UCAS's website editor, explains why the personal statement is such a crucial part of the application form:

A personal statement allows students the chance to stand out of the crowd by telling an institution why they should choose them over someone else with the same grades. It can be one of the most important parts of the application process, so time and care should be taken when filling in this section. It could be the basis for an interview, so students should be prepared to answer questions on it. A student may want to list extra-curricular activities, what career they are working toward and how they will benefit from the degree course that they want to study. They should try to link their hobbies and interests to the skills/experience required for the course.

BEFORE YOU START YOUR PERSONAL STATEMENT

There are a few important things you should think about before you start writing and uploading your personal statement.

1   **Deadlines.** Make a note of exactly when you need to have uploaded your personal statement by. This includes the UCAS application deadline for your course and universities. If you are still in school, college or a sixth form then you may also have extra deadlines for getting help from the staff, or getting things approved by referees.

2   **Start early.** It's better not to rush your statement because it's so important. Leave yourself plenty of time for research, writing, checking and re-drafting.

3   **Make it count.** Your personal statement needs to 'sell' you as a potential undergraduate and help you stand out, so keep that in mind at all times.

4   **Look at good examples.** Find several past examples of successful, well-written statements to get a feel for what's expected.

5   **Prepare well.** Make lots of notes and be ready to write it out several times before it looks right. Try using the checklists that start on page 88 of this chapter so that you don't leave anything important out. Don't upload anything until you're completely happy with it.

6   **Get help.** It's very hard to proofread things on your own. Get help from teachers, advisers, family, and so on, to make sure your personal statement reads well, looks polished, and has no mistakes in it.

WHAT DO ADMISSIONS STAFF WANT TO KNOW?

Some questions from admissions staff at the University of Leicester that a good personal statement should answer:

- What makes you unique, special or impressive?
- What interests you about the course for which you are applying?
- How did you learn about this course/field of work?
- What is your relevant work experience?
- What are your career goals?
- What skills do you have? Can you back your claims up?
- What personal characteristics do you possess? Can you provide evidence?
- What responsibilities have you undertaken?
- What difficulties have you overcome?

MAKING YOUR STATEMENT COUNT

The purpose of writing the personal statement is to make you appealing to one particular target audience: admissions tutors at your chosen institutions. To make it as effective as possible, you should put yourself in their shoes when you're creating the text, and think about what they'd like to learn about you that isn't mentioned elsewhere on the UCAS form.

Tutors want to know that you're genuinely interested in your chosen course, that you understand what the course involves, and that you're capable of doing well academically. You need to show them that you're enthusiastic, motivated and dedicated, and ideally you need to demonstrate that the subject is part of your plans for the future after you've graduated. Aside from the course, they will also want to see some evidence that you'll adjust to a new environment, thrive at college or university, and make a positive contribution to the institution.

The best students show commitment, independence and maturity, and that they have inquiring minds and can think for themselves. Tutors need to know what you're like as a person, and are most likely to select applicants they see as 'well-rounded individuals'. High grades are not enough; they want you to have some 'get up and go', and a life away from your studies as well.

The people who will be reading your personal statement are busy individuals, and each one of them will have their own idea of what's appealing. It's important to understand that there's no accounting for their personal taste, and there's no set or 'perfect' way to craft your statement that can give you 100% assurance of success. All you can do is be true to yourself, prepare it carefully using the pointers in this chapter and give it your best shot.

....

❛ Yeah, found my personal statement a bit of a nightmare to be honest. I got the main bulk of it written over a couple of nights, and then just spent weeks getting it checked by different people and tweaking the wording. The amount of hours I must have spent in total is crazy! I just found it so hard to get everything written in such a small space, and make everything sound good. I got it done eventually though so that's good. My advice is to start early and try not to stress too much! **"**

MATT WILKINSON, AGE 18

WHAT ABOUT COMMERCIAL COMPANIES?

There are companies out there who offer to write or 'improve' your personal statement for you, in return for a fee. Unfortunately, not all of them are reputable, and you might not end up with an original, high-quality statement. While it's understandable that people might be keen to create the best personal statement that they can, there's no guarantee that buying one will ensure admission. Also, the person who knows you best is you – that's why it's called the 'personal statement' in the first place – so other people, especially if they're strangers, are probably not that well suited to writing yours. Remember, at the end of your UCAS application you need to agree to a declaration that states the contents are complete, accurate and all your own work.

RESEARCH

The best place to start is by going back through each of the courses you've decided to apply for. Read the prospectuses and any other related information very carefully; course content and structure are extremely important, as we'll see later. If you're lucky, the websites of the institutions you're applying to may contain specific information about personal statements, and what they're expecting from one. Gather as much information as you can together, so it's all in one place in front of you, and check the admissions criteria.

Think hard about what attracts you to these particular courses, especially if they are subjects that you haven't formally studied yet. Look back at what led to you becoming interested in your subject, and think about ways to show that you'd be a good candidate to study it at a higher level. If you've chosen more than one subject to apply for, ask yourself whether there's one reason in particular why they all appeal, and think very carefully about the things that these diverse courses have in common.

Reading what other people have written

Collect several personal statements together that other students have had success with and compare them. Where possible, look at applications for the subjects that interest you most. You can find examples on the internet, in books, or perhaps from teachers, tutors or careers officers. Study the contents and flow of the text, the running order of the paragraphs, the length and structure of sentences, and the different writing styles and vocabulary of previous students. This should give you a rough idea of what's likely to be successful. While this process should really inform and inspire you, don't be tempted to copy anything in them word-for-word – not even half a sentence. Your statement has to be original: yours, and yours alone.

CHECKLISTS FOR PERSONAL STATEMENTS

Make plenty of background notes before you start writing the personal statement out properly. If certain phrases stand out in course prospectuses or on departmental websites, write them down. The same goes for positive comments that people have made about you, whether in school reports, references for part-time or full-time jobs, and so on. Think about what the course can do for you, and what you can bring to the course and the college or university.

Try answering as many of the questions as you can in the checklists below, but don't worry if you don't have an answer for everything on each list: you're only human and you're not expected to have every single qualification or piece of experience.

Think deeper about the course you've applied for, and write down:

☐ reasons why the course appeals to you
☐ anything you've studied that's related, and how it has led to your interest in the subject
☐ what knowledge you already have about the subject, and how you've developed it
☐ why you would do well studying this subject
☐ elements of the course you're especially interested in – be prepared to go into detail here
☐ personal experiences that have led to your decision to study the subject
☐ how you expect course theory to be put into practice
☐ why the subject is important in the modern world, or everyday life
☐ relevant work experience or placements

- [ ] language skills or previous travel that might be useful for your course
- [ ] other skills, knowledge or experience you have that might help on the course, such as design, model making, mentoring, first aid training, etc.

There is some useful advice at:

www.ucas.com/students/applying/howtoapply/personalstatement/whattoinclude#skills.

Consider all the items in the following academic checklist:

- [ ] your academic experience so far (no need to go into detail if you've already put this information elsewhere on your UCAS application)
- [ ] any special topics you've already studied that have caught your attention, and why they interest you
- [ ] relevant modules, practical work or projects that were especially enjoyable, or that highlight any of your knowledge or talents
- [ ] extra work you've done around the subject, including additional reading and independent research, entering competitions, or having something published or broadcast
- [ ] attending conferences or workshops
- [ ] prizes you have been awarded
- [ ] being part of a programme for gifted students or attending master classes
- [ ] attending summer schools or access courses
- [ ] related key skills, including communication, IT and so on
- [ ] sponsorships or placements you have applied for, or already been awarded
- [ ] courses etc. you have studied that are not accredited, or mentioned elsewhere in the UCAS application
- [ ] memberships or subscriptions
- [ ] evidence that your language skills are good enough to study at university level, if your first language isn't English.

What about your hopes for the future?

- [ ] your main career goal, or what you hope to do after the course
- [ ] other related career goals, and possible specialism at a later date
- [ ] how you think this course will help you reach your career goals
- [ ] what you hope to get out of your time at university.

What you're like as a person:

- ☐ hobbies and interests
- ☐ sports or fitness, other leisure activities
- ☐ full-time or part-time jobs
- ☐ positions of responsibility held at work, in school or college, or in your spare time
- ☐ schemes you are part of: Millennium Volunteers, The Duke of Edinburgh's Award, Young Enterprise, ASDAN Awards, mentoring, sports leadership, local awards and so on
- ☐ voluntary work, community projects, or fundraising
- ☐ teams or societies you are part of
- ☐ prizes you have won at local, county or national level
- ☐ any non-academic achievements
- ☐ skills you have gained from your experiences, such as time management, the ability to work in a team or supervise, dealing with difficult people, working under pressure or to deadlines, being analytical, reasoning and communicating, etc.
- ☐ personal qualities: enthusiasm, reliability, independence, trustworthiness, creativity, and so on
- ☐ major events in your life that have strongly affected you
- ☐ plans for a gap year, if you intend to take one, and how this might relate to your course.

....

When I started writing my personal statement it wasn't going too well, but then some friends said I should get some more advice, so I looked at Studential, Studentroom and the UCAS help pages, and just started working through some of their suggestions. Just get started, write anything – you can always tidy it up or replace it later before you send it. Big yourself up but don't be too bigheaded. ❞

FRANCESCA WINFIELD, AGE 17

WRITING THE FIRST DRAFT

Before you start writing the text of your statement, check with UCAS to make sure you know exactly how the process works, and what's expected of you.

There are basic instructions and Q&As on the website (www.ucas.com), and there's a helpline to call if you get stuck or have software problems (0871 468 0468). Applicants should also have received UCAS booklets, and if you're at school or college your tutors may have created some reference materials of their own to help you.

It's recommended that you type into a word processing program to begin with, not the actual online UCAS form. This is because you should expect to make lots of changes to the statement before it's finally ready. Although it's possible to save and edit your statement online with UCAS without sending it off, you could end up accidentally submitting it before it's ready and after that point you will not be able to make changes to it. It's much better to work on different versions in, for example, MS Word™, and then cut and paste them into the online form at the end when you're happy with everything.

You can write up to 4,000 characters (this includes spaces and punctuation), or 47 lines of text. On average this works out at about 600 words, so you can use that as a rough idea when you're writing your initial draft.

Should you fill all the available space or not? Well, it's a definite case of quality being more important than quantity, and it's best not to pad it out with waffle or comments that are not interesting or relevant. However, it's also an opportunity to make a great case for yourself, so if you can fill out the whole section persuasively and with some flair then you should definitely try to do so. In other words, say what you need to say and then shut up, but it's best if you have a lot of useful things to say.

How can the same statement suit the different places you've applied to?

Remember that, with very few exceptions, the same statement goes out to all your chosen universities and colleges, so you need to be careful what you write to avoid alienating some of them. According to Beth Hayes from UCAS: 'Students can only do one personal statement, which will be sent to all the institutions that they apply to. The likelihood is that applicants will be applying to similar courses, so their personal statement should be tailored towards the type of courses they have applied to. If they apply to more than one course, it's a good idea to focus on the skills and experience required for each course, rather than the subjects. If applicants apply through Extra or Clearing for a different course to their original choices, they should contact the new university or college and ask if they would consider a new personal statement. They can then send a new statement direct to the university or college.'

If you're applying for six similar courses, each at different institutions, the individual universities and colleges will not know who else you've applied to because UCAS doesn't tell them. Keep it that way. Don't mention any of them by name in your personal statement as not only will you put off the ones you *don't* name, you might also look naïve or desperate to the ones you *do* name. Similarly, do not mention course specifics (modules, topics, practical work, work experience etc.) if they are included on some of the courses but not others. It will make admissions tutors think that you don't know much about their course, or that you're not really interested in it, if you get the facts wrong. Only mention items that all the courses have in common.

It gets much trickier if you have decided to apply for courses that are not all similar. You have to be even more careful here so that you don't slip up and give the game away. You might need to talk in more general terms about the subjects without naming them outright, and concentrate on what you have gained overall from your academic and personal experiences. Generally speaking though, the more competition there is for places on a particular course, the less vague you should be if you want to get in. For example, when applying for dual honours degrees, be aware that some admissions tutors will not look kindly on you if you fail to mention both components of the degree. Take plenty of time when wording your statement if you're looking at a number of dual honours degrees which don't have similar titles. Failing that, you might have to go with wording that's tailored to fit your top few choices, but that might appear less specific to tutors at your less favoured institutions. Or you might decide to be open about it, and explain clearly why you have applied to different courses.

Do none of your chosen courses have much in common? If that's the case, consider revisiting the choices you have made, especially if it's making your personal statement look hopelessly vague. It could be worth going back a few steps and rethinking what you want to study, and coming back with something that looks more coherent and decisive. After all, admissions staff want to see strong interest and motivation, so make sure that's how you feel. Don't rush into making applications if you aren't sure about them.

Writing tips for style

There is no 'right' or 'wrong' way to write a personal statement, but many admissions tutors say that they expect the majority of the text to be about why you want to do the course, and why you will do well on it. Therefore this is the area you should concentrate on the hardest. Some say you should devote at least 50% of the space to this, and others prefer around 75%. The remaining text should be about your interests, hobbies, personality etc., and your plans for the future.

However you decide to structure your personal statement, it needs to read smoothly and have a logical flow to it. Because of the lack of space, most students break their text up into paragraphs, and some also use short sub-headings. Each paragraph must leave the reader wanting to know more and link into the paragraph below. The most common structure is an essay-style format as follows, although you don't have to stick to it.

1 Opening paragraph: usually about why you have chosen to study this subject at university, and what interests you about it.

2 Your related academic interests and ability, and other supporting evidence that you will do well on this course and at university.

3 Relevant hobbies and interests, responsibilities, and what kind of person you are.

4 Closing paragraph about why you want to come to university, what you hope to gain from the degree, and your career plans.

A carefully written first paragraph is an absolute must. You want to grab the reader's attention right away, for all the right reasons. This will then help to hold their eye throughout the rest of the statement so they don't simply skim through it, and a good first impression helps them to remember you in preference to the rest of the competition. Most tutors recommend that your first paragraph should be about why you're interested in the subject you want to study. You won't get it right first time, so let go and turn out as many ideas as you can come up with, however crazy some of them might seem at the time. It's worth writing a handful of alternative beginnings, comparing them with the opening paragraphs of successful previous applications, and then picking your most convincing one after you've allowed some time for reflection.

Many budding writers are taught that if they want their material to be interesting they should 'show, and don't tell'. This is also true for your statement. Admissions staff want to know how your experiences have taught and shaped you and why certain subjects grab your interest, and they expect to read examples that demonstrate your commitment, instead of being given a list of dry facts. Rather than bluntly stating, 'I am hard working and reliable', or, 'I'm interested in politics', you'd be much better off providing supporting evidence for these statements: for example, 'My part time job in a busy store has taught me the importance of time management and teamwork', or, 'Setting up the school debating society has given me the opportunity to explore many topical issues in greater depth'.

Deliberately pick dynamic, positive language to use in your sentences: achieved, joined, involved, goal, experience, training, planning, volunteering, and so on. Likewise, avoid negative language such as: terrible, useless, mistake, hated, never, can't, etc. However, you can include phrases about 'overcoming difficulties', 'taking on challenges', or 'learning valuable lessons'.

It's best to avoid 'purple prose' – overblown, over-emotive language – unless you're applying for the kind of course where flamboyance is actively encouraged. Most of the time it makes you look slightly insane, pretentious and somewhat insincere.

Sylvia Zalk, Programme Officer at Imperial College, London has some interesting stories to tell about personal statements.

....

❝ When I worked at another university I did get an amusingly slushy personal statement from a student: "Walking by a babbling brook I saw a beautiful butterfly. Its wing was broken. It made me so sad that I could do nothing to ease its suffering that I shed a tear. At that point I decided to study biomedical sciences at this college."

Actually, someone has trumped the butterfly personal statement. Yesterday I saw a personal statement from a student where she started by talking about her entire childhood, and went through to losing her virginity and how this has affected her as an artist. It was a pile of pretentious piffle. Apart from making herself look mad, the garbled, irrelevant nature of it all immediately disqualified her, as she was applying for a communications course. I'd say KEEP TO THE POINT! Also don't try and be witty. Academics look for a succinct personal statement in my experience. 🥢

Do:

- be selective and pick what's relevant
- prioritise, if it doesn't all fit in to the space allowed
- be concise and use plain English
- keep it structured and use paragraphs
- keep it interesting
- be open and honest
- use positive and enthusiastic language
- back up comments with examples
- be prepared to talk about what you've written.

Don't:

- give your entire life story
- start every sentence with 'I' or 'My'
- make jokes or be pretentious
- try too hard to be quirky
- use long words that you'd never normally use
- make things up or lie
- express strong political views
- repeat material you have elsewhere on the form
- waffle just to fill up the space.

When you're writing about leisure interests and hobbies, try not to go for the same things that everyone else might mention, such as 'watching football', 'reading' or 'socialising'. Something a bit more unusual will stand out, such as playing the tuba in a brass band, or learning how to tango. Pick things that link in with the course in some way, wherever possible. You should also mention any transferable skills your hobbies have helped to build up. If all your hobbies are fairly generic try to show that you're accomplished in some way, such as captaining the hockey team, organising large events, or being awarded the highest grade for playing the piano. This is not the time to mention that you spend most of your free time in the pub or online gossiping with friends on social media, or taking part in magical fantasy role-playing games.

It's best to explain anything on your statement that stands out. Sometimes applicants have to write about negative things, such as illness or bereavement, that has affected their predicted grades, family commitments that have affected their choices, or a life event that has made them alter their plans. Wherever possible, try to include a positive note, such as a mention of your determination to succeed, or that you have gained life experience or re-evaluated your priorities.

If you're planning to take a gap year, you could comment on this towards the end of your statement. If possible, explain why you're taking it and what you hope to achieve, especially if it links in with your studies in some way. For example, you might wish to work to help fund your studies, do some community work, travel, or learn new skills or languages. Probably best not to mention if you're just planning on sunbathing and partying on a beach in Thailand for the whole year though. Deferral for a gap year is mentioned elsewhere on the application form so you could leave this out, but you should be prepared to answer questions about it.

Just as it's vital to open your personal statement in style, it's equally important to close it well. The best closing paragraphs tie everything up neatly, reaffirming your interest in the chosen degree, and most of them sum up the student's goals relating to the course. This is a good time to mention how you hope your higher education will fit in with your plans for life after university or college, if you haven't done so in the first paragraph. Again, readers tend to strongly remember a closing paragraph, so you might like to write several versions of it and then pick your favourite one. You can ask other people, such as relatives, teachers, or friends which version they prefer, but remember that ultimately the decision is yours.

International students

If you're hoping to study as an international student you should explain why you've chosen the UK for your studies, and you also need to demonstrate good language skills. This means creating a well-written statement, and providing some other evidence to prove you can study a course taught in English. For example, it might be useful to mention previous travel to the UK or another English-speaking nation, or part time work as a translator or in a call centre, and so on.

Mature students

Students who are not currently in education can draw on their working lives for inspiration. Write about your current and past jobs and what you have gained from them, as there may be many transferable skills – anything from managing projects to taking the initiative when researching and evaluating new areas. You'll also need to write persuasively about why you have now become interested in entering higher education. If the degree will lead to a career change, explain why this is what you want.

USING QUOTES

Some admissions tutors like to see interesting quotes in a personal statement and others dislike them very much. A well-chosen quote can catch the reader's eye and make a statement unique, so sometimes they can fit well in an opening paragraph, for example. If you're going to quote anyone, make sure you use the correct punctuation and attribute the quote to them. It's also important to make sure that you've quoted them exactly, or else your mistake could leave you looking silly. Avoid filling your statement up with a very long wordy quote, or several smaller ones, as it takes up too much space and means that you will have less room for describing yourself in your own words, so tutors won't get enough of an idea of what you're like as a person. If in doubt, don't use quotes.

PLAGIARISM AND DISHONESTY

It's very important to avoid copying other people's work when you're writing, as plagiarism can lose you a place at university. Admissions tutors read hundreds of applications, and often spot over-used or directly copied phrases, which they do not look upon favourably. Now there's an even more effective way to catch out cheating students: UCAS's Similarity Detection software. If you're tempted to copy as little as half a sentence or one phrase from another student's personal statement, there's a very good chance you will be discovered. Taking whole sentences or paragraphs and slightly rewriting them can also get you reported. According to UCAS's Beth Hayes: 'UCAS does have very efficient plagiarism software. If the software detects similarities then UCAS will send the results to the institutions that the applicant has applied to, and from then on it is up to the institutions' discretion on what they want to do.

'It is important that students don't copy personal statements from other people or from the internet, primarily because they will be found out which could in turn lead to them losing a place at their chosen institutions. The personal statement is 'personal' – it should be written by the applicant in their own style. This is the only way that admissions tutors get to know them as a person before an interview. If they are offered an interview, they will probably be asked to elaborate on the information they have provided, and it is very obvious to admissions tutors when students are not speaking from personal experience.'

Some students lie in their personal statements to sound more knowledgeable, experienced, or interesting. Be warned though, talking yourself up a bit is one thing, but an outright lie can badly backfire. Some institutions might ask for documented proof of some of your claims before they'll offer you a place. Anything that stands out in your application can become a target for in-depth questions during an interview, leaving you floundering.

Don't be like the hapless student who lied and claimed they could play the sitar to make their application to medical school look unique. Yes, you've guessed it, his main interviewer turned out to be a doctor who really was a classically trained sitar player, and asked several awkward musical questions that the student couldn't answer. So, while you might not end up in trouble for bending the truth a little, outright lies can easily catch up with you.

CHECKING AND RE-DRAFTING

Once you've put together a rough first draft you can start to check it through and begin to refine it. Read it very slowly to yourself a few times, and make a note of anything that you want to keep or change. Imagine that you're an admissions tutor who needs to be impressed when you're reading it. Make sure each different point in the personal statement links together logically, and then try reading it out loud to yourself to see whether it has a pleasing style and an interesting flow. Save each new draft as a separate document in case you edit out anything that you decide you want to add back in later, and keep backup copies of these files. Keep making changes until you're reasonably happy.

If the word count is too high, you will have to take steps to trim it down. Go back and cut out any repetition and waffling, then see whether you can turn some of it into shorter, simpler sentences. If it's still way over the character count, ask a teacher or careers adviser to help you trim it down – an English teacher might be best at this. You can also ask your referee to write about some of the things they are going to mention in their own statement, saving you more space.

The next step is to thoroughly go through the whole document to check the spelling, punctuation and grammar. A spell-checker will not pick up all mistakes, so you have to do this yourself with a dictionary to hand. After you've gone through it a couple of times you can even try reading it backwards, as your eyes might have become tired and this can help spot individual spelling mistakes that you might otherwise have skimmed over and missed. Take special care when mentioning the names of authors, or the titles of articles or books, as errors can make you appear ill-informed or sloppy.

Get someone else to read it and give you an honest appraisal, or ideally ask a few people – including teachers, careers advisers, parents and friends. Ask them to check for mistakes, to tell you what's working well, and to look for anything you might have missed out. Don't be shy. You can post it on some student websites too and ask for comments, but be aware that it might get stolen (potentially leaving *you* accused of plagiarism), and the advice you get might not be particularly accurate or constructive. If your readers do come up with useful ideas, incorporate them into the statement, redraft it as many times as needed, then go back again and thoroughly check the grammar and spelling. If possible, get some more second opinions and help looking for mistakes this time as well. Eventually you will have your final draft. If you have time, put it to one side for a couple of days to gain some perspective then read it through once more to make sure it represents you and your goals.

> ❝ My personal statement was hard at first because my advisers told me that the first paragraph must be spectacular in order to get the reader (admissions tutor) interested, so I wasted a lot of time trying to make the first paragraph fantastic. And the fact that I had a lot of A level revision to do made me forget about the personal statement at times. But when I did finish it I had it checked numerous times by my institution for any minor mistakes, so overall I was pleased with it. However I want to say that the personal statement system is actually ineffective in some circumstances. For example, if you want to apply to two different courses that are similar in content (e.g. chemistry and biology) you have to generalise your personal statement to fit the criteria. ❞
>
> **MAHAMED ABUKAR, STUDYING A LEVELS AT HAMMERSMITH AND WEST LONDON COLLEGE**

FILLING THE STATEMENT IN ONLINE

You should now be ready to format and upload your personal statement to UCAS. Go to the website and enter your username and password, then open up the Apply system. Copy and paste your word-processed document into Apply. Apply times out after a few minutes of inactivity, so make sure you save your text during this time otherwise it could be lost.

Be aware that bold text, italics, underlining and foreign characters will be removed when you save the text. Even 'curly' quotation marks (the slanted ones seen in some Microsoft Word fonts), indentations at the beginning of paragraphs, tabs, multiple spaces and long dashes get removed.

After saving the pasted document remember to check it all through once more to make sure nothing has gone wrong with the formatting, and tidy it up if needed. In particular look for lines of text getting broken at strange points, which will eat up space and look messy. Make sure you have not exceeded 4,000 characters or 47 lines, whichever is the shorter, and remember that 47 lines includes any empty lines between paragraphs too. Each time you save the document, the characters and lines will be automatically counted for you, so it's easy to keep track.

> ❝ I did my original statement on a word processing program first, made it perfect there, and then just copied and pasted it into the Apply system. That was it really, although I did have to edit it once, but that only took a couple of seconds. I do have to say though, there is a limit on both the amount of lines you can use in your personal statement, and the number of letters. They [UCAS] should use one or the other, because at first I had the right number of letters used, but it went over too many lines. It meant that I still had to delete things out of my original personal statement. ❞
>
> **CORINNE RILEY, AGE 18, CHEADLE AND MARPLE SIXTH FORM COLLEGE**

AFTER YOU'VE FINISHED UPLOADING

Once the statement's uploaded, you need to agree to the declaration that it's all your own original work. If you're applying via school or college, you now have to send the application to your referee. If you're applying independently, you cut and paste your referee's comments into Apply, fill in their details and send the application to UCAS yourself (see Chapter 4).

Print copies of your personal statement off to refer to in case you are called to interview, or have to go through Clearing and need to refresh your memory quickly. It is often the basis for some very searching questions.

After your application arrives with UCAS, and is forwarded on to the institutions you've chosen, you'll start to receive offers and/or rejections (see Chapter 7). You may also be asked to attend an interview, or to do tests (see Chapter 6).

UCAS will also send you a welcome letter that includes your application number, personal ID number and username for Track, and the list of your course choices. If this letter hasn't arrived within 14 days of submitting your application then contact UCAS.

Changing a personal statement after you've uploaded it

If you make one or two small mistakes, it's easy enough to use the Apply software to change the saved document. Should there be any problems, you can ring the UCAS customer service line for help. Once the application's been sent off though, you won't be able to change it. This can be a problem for students who decide to apply for new types of course via Extra, Clearing or Adjustment – if you find yourself in any of these situations then your personal statement might not match up with your new course. If that's the case, you may decide to create a new personal statement and send it separately to support your new applications.

SUMMARY:
EFFECTIVE PERSONAL STATEMENTS

1. Remember deadlines. Allow plenty of time for getting your statement ready: it's not something that you should rush at the last minute. Make a note of UCAS application deadlines, and make sure you know when school staff or referees need material from you.

2. Think who's reading it. Your statement must explain to admissions officers why you want to study this subject, why you will do well academically, and show that you're mature and responsible enough to adapt to university life.

3. Research and reflect. Take plenty of time to prepare, and make notes before you begin writing. Make sure you know all the course details, and think of ways to demonstrate your interest in the course and generally show yourself in a good light.

4. Pick your words carefully. Use plain English, have a good opening and closing paragraph, employ positive language, sound dynamic and interesting, and provide evidence that you have the right range of skills, talents and experience. Don't waffle or mention unrelated details. Don't limit your chances by mentioning names of institutions or course components that are not available.

5. Don't cheat, don't lie. Plagiarism is increasingly easy to spot, so don't risk it. Outright lies tend to come back to haunt you later. Both will lose you a place at college or university.

6. Keep re-writing. The first draft always needs more work. Keep editing until it's polished, and read it out loud to see if it's convincing. Putting it aside for a day or so can also give some perspective and show up areas that need changing.

7. Ask for opinions. However embarrassing it might be, you need to show it to a few other people. Include at least one person who works in education. They might think of something important you've missed out, or help you with phrasing or getting the word count right.

8. Check, check, check. Admissions tutors will quickly spot any mistakes with spelling and grammar. Errors in your writing make you look careless and sloppy, so you must make the effort to look like you can cut it in an academic environment.

9. Upload it properly. Cut and paste from a word processor into the online Apply form. After saving, check the number of characters or lines, and make sure no errors have been introduced into the formatting.

10. Keep a copy. You will need to refer back to your personal statement if you are invited for an interview, as it's likely to form the basis of many of the questions.

CHAPTER SIX
SELECTION INTERVIEWS AND TESTS

You are likely to be interviewed at least once if you apply for vocational courses such as dentistry, medicine or teacher training, or if you hope to attend prestigious institutions such as colleges in Cambridge or Oxford. The majority of applicants are not invited to attend an interview, but if you are asked to have one then this is good news – it usually means that you fulfil the entry criteria and the university would like to know more about you as a person. While this can all be a little nerve-wracking, it's good to know that careful preparation can improve your chances of success.

The future of interviews is uncertain in light of recent high levels of applications. Some people think there will be fewer interviews as university staff may end up with limited time or resources to deal with all the applications, and will therefore make decisions based on UCAS applications and personal statements. Others have suggested that there will be too many applicants with identical predicted grades and similar applications, so interviews will become more common. Yet others believe that universities will become more likely to ask candidates to sit tests or supply extra material along with their applications.

SUCCEEDING AT INTERVIEW

Interviewers will be looking for:

- **Attitude**: interest and enthusiasm, commitment, motivation
- **Personality**: usually someone pleasant and reasonably mature whom they will enjoy teaching
- **Intellectual attributes**: able to concentrate and think clearly, pick up new ideas quickly, think independently, be analytical and critical, and apply existing knowledge to new situations
- **Suitability**: whether you are an appropriate student who is suited to the course, and is likely to do well on it.

While most of the focus will be academic and you must show you understand what studying the subject entails, they also want well rounded candidates who will contribute to the university as a whole, rather than course-obsessed geeks who stay in their room reading for the next few years. Be interesting as well as interested.

On the more competitive courses, an interview can sometimes be the best way to stand out and win that coveted place, as everyone else who's applied will probably also have top grades, the 'right' work experience, and a very well written personal statement.

....

❝ I was unbelievably nervous before my first interview, which was at Manchester Uni. Beforehand I was worried in case they asked me something complicated about a subject I don't know anything about; I suppose I was scared I would look stupid. Afterward, I came out thinking it was reasonably easy. It lasted less than 10 minutes and it was very informal. **❞**

BECKY, AGE 17

WHAT TO EXPECT

Selection or admissions interviews vary from institution to institution, and from department to department. The list below is therefore a very rough guide to what to expect from the process.

1   Offers of interviews arrive (usually via UCAS Track)

2   Confirm your attendance and ask for more details

3   Prepare for interview

4   Travel to interview in plenty of time

5   Attend one or more interviews, and hopefully make a good impression

6   Possibly sit tests or supply additional material (dates vary for this)

7   Return home and wait for decision (usually via Track)

8   Receive a possible offer, or get feedback on possible rejection

Universities now make most of their invitations via UCAS Track. You will be sent an email or text alert from the site to let you know the message has arrived, and then you can log in to find out the exact details. You have the options to accept or decline interviews, and to request an alternative time or date.

There are several types of interview and it can be less daunting if you know beforehand about the format it's going to be in. Most commonly, interviews are one-to-one with a tutor, or you will be interviewed by a small panel of staff, one of whom often takes notes. The usual length of a university admissions interview is somewhere between 15 and 40 minutes, although this can vary. You may sometimes be invited to a background session before the proper interview, where the process is explained to you, and you can pick up some useful tips about what the interviewers are looking for.

You could be asked to come in for an 'informal' interview, or be asked to do a telephone interview. Less commonly, you may be invited to attend a group interview with one or more other students, or – in the creative arts – to show your portfolio or perform an audition. You may also be asked to bring extra materials with you, such as recent essays or projects, or to take admissions or aptitude tests.

Who is most likely to hold interviews?

Interviews are frequently held for vocational courses and other competitive subjects, including veterinary science, dentistry and medicine. Oxford and Cambridge colleges frequently interview the great majority of applicants who fit their entry criteria.

When are different interviews held?

Make a note of when interviews for your chosen subjects, colleges and universities are most likely to be held.

- The earlier candidates apply, the earlier they may be interviewed
- Oxford and Cambridge interviews are held in December, with the possibility of more in January
- Many universities mention their most common interview dates on their websites, and this information is often mentioned in the course entry profiles on www.ucas.com

If you know you're applying to courses where you think there's a strong chance of candidates being interviewed, try not to be unavailable during the interview period. Although some institutions are happy to reschedule admissions interviews around exams or illness, or following bereavements, it's unrealistic to expect them to wait for you to come back from that fortnight in Ibiza. If there is a problem with the timing of an interview, let the university know as soon as possible so they have plenty of time to find an alternative date.

HOW TO DO WELL AT INTERVIEW

Although it may be slightly daunting, the offer of an interview is generally an encouraging sign. It's far better than getting an outright 'Application unsuccessful' showing up in your Track shortly after you've sent your form off. If one or more colleges or universities invite you to attend an interview then they already see you as a good potential candidate, at least on paper, and want to meet you to find out more.

Confirming

Once the offer of an interview arrives, read the small print and make sure you're not doing anything else on that day, before clearly noting it down in your diary or organiser. Then confirm via Track that you'll be attending. It can also be helpful to call their admissions office if you have any questions: for example, you might need to ask about the interview format, and if you have a long journey you should also ask about how to book accommodation for the night before the interview. Check whether or not you need to bring anything else with you, such as examples of your work, or whether you should be expecting something extra, such as an aptitude test. If you have any disabilities or special needs, now is a good time to mention this to give the university plenty of notice so that they can make the necessary arrangements.

> Pre-university interview nerves are completely normal and it is OK to feel nervous. Whether you are 18 or 38, the key is preparation. Firstly, this means understanding WHY you have chosen this path, this university and your degree, and being honest about it.

Get familiar with the journey, do the obvious things like open days and if you can, go to departmental summer tasters. Plus an informal visit can sometimes be more revealing than planned ones. Try focusing on positives and remember everyone is in the same boat (though some people are better than others at concealing how they feel). Over-confidence can be risky at interviews. 〟

NAOMI ELFRED, CONNEXIONS PERSONAL ADVISER

Preparing

There are some people who will tell you that you cannot prepare for a university interview, but that is not entirely correct. While it is true that you cannot anticipate exactly what questions you are most likely to be asked, there is plenty of groundwork you can still do to help yourself, and make sure you arrive feeling relatively confident. For example you can:

- refresh your memory about the course you've applied to
- research the department and staff
- review your coursework
- go back through your extra reading
- re-read your application
- pick out a good interview outfit
- arrange your travel and accommodation
- take a mock interview
- read up on general interview skills
- look at tips specific to your subject or university/college
- think of questions you'd like answering
- pack your bag and get ready to set off.

Most admissions staff will tell you that when students have done little or no background work, it really shows and doesn't create a good impression at all. So where do you start? Perhaps one of the best places to begin is with the course itself, and remembering what it was that attracted you to it in the first place. Go back through the prospectus and course structure and remind yourself of the specifics, as one of the most important parts of the interview will be your enthusiasm for the particular course itself, as well as your ability to demonstrate an interest in the overall subject.

It's also a good idea to recap your knowledge of the department or school you hope to study at, and look at their well-known areas of research and any other strengths. Start by looking at their website. Key members of staff may have written important academic articles, reviews or textbooks, or been in the press recently. You don't need to become an expert on their work, just read a synopsis here and there, or be generally aware of what they do.

Flick through any recent coursework you have completed in the last few months, if you are at school or doing an access course, etc. Is there any particular subject, topic or subtopic that has caught your interest? You might well be asked about your favourite areas of study, so be prepared to answer questions about them. In particular, you might be asked about wider reading that you've done in relation to your studies, as this shows an enquiring mind and the ability to manage your own learning, rather than reading only what your school gave you.

If you've mentioned any extra reading in your application, you had better know what you're talking about! It's very likely that you will be quizzed on it, and asked to give an opinion. If it's a well-known text, for example, refresh your memory of it, and perhaps read one or more reviews or evaluations to get you thinking about it. Once you've checked through your application form, look at your personal statement once more. You must be ready to back up any statements you've made in it, or to talk enthusiastically about your work experience and interests.

Read around the subject and think about how it is part of everyday life. In particular, keep up to date with the current affairs and look for elements of your subject in the broadsheet newspapers, relevant magazines or journals, in radio or television news or documentaries, or on news or leading industry websites.

If the subject you want to study is not one that's available at A level, like geoscience or nursing for example, you will not be expected to answer technical questions about it. However, you will need to demonstrate an awareness of the subject in the wider world, and have a rough idea of possible career structures and current issues.

‘ I had only one interview and thought I'd mucked it up sooo badly; the nerves got to me big time. I stumbled on words, repeated myself, kept apologising. My answers were too short, not specific enough. But the interviewers were quite nice, I suppose they see a lot of nervous students, and they helped me along a bit and were patient. ’

AI, AGE 17

WHAT DO I WEAR?

It's often hard to work out what to wear for an interview, but for most places you won't need to go for a suit. The most important factor is comfort, as you may be wearing the outfit for the whole day and possibly travelling in it, but it needs to be smart as well. Most of the time it's best to go for the dreaded 'smart casual', so that's trousers (or smart skirt) and a shirt or blouse, and a pair of new-ish and clean shoes. Jeans and trainers are best avoided, although if that's how you're the most confident and you feel you have to pick them, at least make sure they're clean and ironed. Break shoes in a little beforehand so you're not getting blisters during the interview, and check you've removed tags, pins and packaging from new shirts or blouses. Leave the big jangly jewellery at home because it's too distracting, and if you have long hair think about tying it back to keep it tidy. If your interview is in the winter months, make sure you have layers of clothing for extra warmth so you don't arrive shivering. Lay everything out before you go to bed on the night before the interview to save time and stress the following morning. Consider buying a new file to hold any important paperwork and keep it tidy, so you don't have to shuffle papers around when you're trying to find things.

Make sure you know exactly when and where your interview is taking place, as the campus might be quite spread out and it's easy to go to the wrong building. Plan your journey and route, and allow plenty of time for arrival. It's not uncommon to be plagued by delayed trains, broken-down buses or roadworks, so build that into your plans, and take the department's contact details with you so that you can phone ahead should you experience serious problems. Print off road, town and campus maps if the department hasn't already supplied these, and don't rely completely on a smartphone for this as there may be problems with reception.

If you are planning an overnight stay, arrange your accommodation well in advance, and see whether the university has any 'student ambassadors' who will meet you and show you around the campus and the town to give you a student's-eye view of the place. However, be careful not to get too drunk if you go out on the town, as a hangover will be easy to spot and will impair your performance at the interview the following day.

A mock or practice interview can be an extremely helpful way to build up your confidence before you set off for the real interview. Ask school or college staff, or a careers adviser, about setting one up and ask them for constructive feedback so that you can tackle any possible weak spots.

If you have time, consider brushing up on general interview skills. A variety of books and websites can give you tips on presenting yourself, making a good impression, handling your nerves, using positive body language, and coping with tricky questions and situations. Try *Young Jobhunters: Interview Skills* by Helen Cooper and *You're Hired! Interview* by Judi James (both published by Trotman) and *Perfect Interview* by Max Eggert (published by Random House), or ask an adviser to suggest something from their careers library.

You could also seek out tips specific to undergraduate interviews in your subject at your chosen university or college. Internet message boards on www.yougo. co.uk and www.thestudentroom.co.uk are also places to try a search or to pose a question to students who have been through the experience before you. Users will be able to give you a rough idea of questions, although you will have to 'think on your feet' on the day as the exact questions are unlikely to come up.

COMMON QUESTIONS

Think about how you might answer the commonest interview questions, such as the following.

- Why do you want to do this course?
- How did you become interested in this subject?

- Which part of the course interests you the most?
- What's the most interesting thing you're studying at the moment?
- What qualities do you think you need to do well in this subject?
- What attracts you to this university?
- Have you done any relevant work experience?
- What do you know about this current news story?
- What are your views on this controversial issue?
- Tell me about your hobbies.
- What are your future career intentions?

Try to keep your answers positive and enthusiastic, and don't write them down and learn them word-for-word or parrot-fashion – in a real interview they will sound over-rehearsed and not genuine.

Come up with some sensible questions you can ask at the end of your interview to show your interest in learning the subject or finding out more about the university. Don't ask about things you already know are on the department's website or in the prospectus, or you'll look ignorant – ask about something else that's not covered in detail, such as tutorial support, links with industry, mentoring, the scope of project work, or ask about prospects after graduating. Again, don't memorise your questions word for word, or you'll sound stilted to the interviewers. Have at least one or two roughly prepared, or perhaps three, but don't overdo it.

All that remains is for you to pack your bag and get ready to set off. Include letters, maps, transport times, a copy of your application form and personal statement, a prospectus, extra material they've asked you to supply, and any preparatory notes you've made. Use a small neat folder to keep it organised if you can. You'll also need to pack railcards, tickets, mobile phone, cash for snacks and drinks, something to read if you end up waiting, and maybe an umbrella. Store any important numbers in your phone. Set your alarm clock to get up in plenty of time, lay out your interview clothes, charge up your mobile, and try to get an early night.

Arriving at the interview

Timing is important. If you're more than 15 minutes early, walk around the campus or look at your notes so you're not hanging around too long in the waiting area. If you're running late for whatever reason, call ahead and apologise profusely (even if it's not your fault), and ask whether they'd be kind enough to wait for you. Otherwise, aim to arrive about 10 to 15 minutes before the start of the interview, introduce yourself politely to the receptionist or support staff, then go off and freshen up. Check your hair and teeth, and straighten up your clothes. If you have sweaty palms, wipe them with a tissue. Take a couple of deep breaths if you're feeling nervous and try to relax. Remind yourself that a little anxiety can actually improve your performance during an interview. Then go back to the waiting area until you are called in. Don't chew gum or eat while you're waiting, and be absolutely certain that your mobile phone is switched off.

☑ TIP

Tutors sometimes ask receptionists to keep an eye on the candidates who are waiting, and mention who's particularly pleasant (or not). It pays to be nice. Also, these are people you might end up on a course with in the next few months.

When you are called into the interview room, remember that first impressions count. Stand up straight, say hello, make eye contact with the interviewer(s), smile and shake hands with people as they introduce themselves. Try to remember their names, and wait to be offered a seat before sitting down. Try not to fidget or slouch, and if your hands are a bit shaky from nerves then fold them lightly on your lap. Avoid sitting with your arms and legs crossed, and if possible, lean slightly forwards to show interest in what the interviewer says. Try to look keen and confident, rather than uninterested, cocky or arrogant.

☑ TIP

If you feel slightly anxious, try not to worry too much as the interviewers are probably well used to dealing with stressed out students, and they won't hold it against you.

The interview itself

Most interviewers are kind, and will ask you a few general warm-up questions. Think about what you are going to say, rather than blurting out the first thing that comes into your head, and take your time. Try to give whole answers, and if possible, avoid trailing off leaving an unfinished sentence. Don't waffle or try to bluff your way through anything you clearly know nothing about, as you may be asked an even more complicated follow-up question that leaves you totally floundering.

It's quite possible that an interviewer will ask you a question that you don't fully understand or have an answer to. If so, don't be scared to ask them to repeat the question, or to explain part of it to you. If it's a topic you haven't studied yet, be honest and say so. Sometimes there is no 'right' or 'wrong' answer to a question, and they are simply interested in finding out the way you approach a problem and think it through, or how well you can understand the complex components of an issue. Sometimes the best answer comes in two parts: what you think about something, followed by an explanation of your opinions. If the interviewer questions your opinion, be prepared to defend it logically as this is where you might score bonus points.

Remember that they are not trying to 'trick' you, or humiliate you – but do be prepared for some tougher questions to come later. They may wish to see how you react under pressure, and how well you are concentrating. Just take your time and try not to get flustered. Sometimes the interviewers might prompt you a little if you slow down or get slightly stuck during an answer, but don't worry, this can often be a good sign and suggests they want to hear more of what you've got to say.

You will probably be asked about some of your hobbies, interests and extra-curricular activities too, because they're looking for personality and character as well. Remember to be enthusiastic when talking about them.

☑ **TIP**

If you are being interviewed by more than one person, make eye contact mainly with the person who has asked you the most recent question.

The end of the interview

This is a good opportunity to ask some of the questions you researched earlier. Try to keep it academic rather than social if you can, to show interest in the department and the course. Once this is over, take your cues from the interviewers, who will probably say goodbye and thank you and show you out. Make sure that you say 'thank you' as well before you leave.

TELEPHONE INTERVIEWS

If you are offered a telephone interview, take it as seriously as if you'd been invited to attend an interview in person. Start by doing your background research as mentioned earlier in this chapter, and have your personal statement and a few questions ready. Find somewhere quiet to take the call so that you won't be interrupted, and make sure there's as little background noise as possible. Although you can't impress the interviewer's eyes with a smart outfit or clever use of body language, you can still use a number of tricks to create a good impression: sit up straight in a chair, have your paperwork arranged tidily on a table or desk in front of you, and smile from time to time (it can improve the tone of your voice and helps you to relax). Don't drink, smoke, snack or chew gum. Take your time when answering any questions, think things through before speaking, and ask first if there's anything you don't understand. However nervous you are, try to speak up and avoid talking in a monotonous voice. Say 'thank you' for the interviewer's time at the end, and let them be the first to hang up. You may find it useful to jot down a few notes about the conversation after the interview is over.

Martin Thompson, Head of Initial Teacher Training at the Pilgrim Partnership in Bedfordshire, gives some tips on what interviewers might be looking out for.

❝On an application form we would want to see all the details asked for, well presented with good use of standard English (remember the use of ICT is an important skill for teaching, so if electronically presented it should show their competence/expertise with this). We also look for genuine interest in working with/ being around children who are not family members, i.e. Brownie leader, football coach, etc., because experience in schools is not always easy to achieve, whereas such activities are open to all (suitable) interested parties. Also, teachers have to be prepared to give of themselves and such voluntary work is a good indicator of this.*

During an interview they must try to engage with the panel, be suitably (but not alarmingly) enthusiastic, and concise in their answers (weaker ones often tend to be too long and ramble). We look for flexibility and no hint of awkwardness (I thought this would happen, I didn't expect etc.), and in needing team players we are looking for people who get on with others, particularly with fellow candidates. The ability to be self-reflective, concisely, is important. We ask what they will enjoy most and what they will enjoy least as part of testing whether they have a realistic view of the profession. Also answers to what being part of a profession, rather than just a job, means are often not good and very few can express how being in a profession might show itself within the ordinary working day.

*If they ask questions when prompted at the end, which we like and encourage, the questions shouldn't be about things they should already know, or could have found out. We also worry a bit about those who, once they have accepted a place, make too many phone calls etc. asking for sometimes rather petty things. There is a tendency for trainees from recent years to be very demanding, and you would expect them to be able to deal with some of these requests themselves, so they can be inadvertently giving negative indicators of their potential.**"**

INFORMAL INTERVIEWS

Some interviews are described as 'informal', in that they are not meant to appear intimidating, but you should be aware that your performance in an informal interview can still affect your chances of being offered a place. It's better to take it seriously, so re-read your course information and application, and prepare some questions beforehand. Informal interviews sometimes take place during open days and tours of departments, and are an excellent opportunity to find out more about an institution.

SPECIFIC INSTITUTIONS AND COURSES

- If you're applying for medicine, law, or other vocational courses, then expect to be asked questions about your work experience, and anything else that shows your understanding of, and commitment to, a future career.
- Modern language interviews are often conducted entirely or partly in that language to assess your general conversational skills and vocabulary, and you might be asked to complete a written grammar test as well.
- Applicants to Oxford or Cambridge can expect two or three interviews, which may include an extra interview at a college to which they didn't apply. If they don't get into their college of choice they may be recalled for interview and/or placed in a pool of applicants for spare places.

❝ I went for uninterview to read law at a certain Oxford college. I had to sit entrance exams before the interviews. I'd had a rather nasty accident the weekend prior to the exams, and was on a liquid diet when I sat them. The upshot of this was that my school sent a covering letter with my exams, explaining that my performance may have been affected accordingly.**"**

"I was invited to my first choice college to attend two interviews some weeks later. As these were spread over two days, with the possibility of being invited to a second or third choice college thereafter, I was offered accommodation in the college for my stay. The building I stayed in was fairly modern, with lights that switched on in the kitchen and corridor areas when you opened the doors (coming from a comprehensive school in South Wales, I am very easily impressed). By contrast, the interviews were held in grandiose rooms lined with volumes upon volumes of books, in an attractive eighteenth-century quadrangle. This was admittedly a little intimidating. By "a little", I of course mean "a lot".**"**

"My terror (yes, it's fair to say that it was terror) was mostly assuaged by my first interviewer, who was warm and engaging. I did remain a little edgy, however – as a younger, sharp-featured lady was perched nearby in watchful silence. The fellow excitedly enquired about my accident – how it happened, and whether I was going to pursue legal action. Although I wouldn't recommend running into a tensed wire to anyone, it did occur to me that it might prove to be a blessing – albeit a remarkably painful one. And indeed, talking about it would subsequently eclipse the majority of time given for both interviews.**"**

'Towards the end of the first interview, I was given a handout which documented (to the best of my recollection) a few situations in which an action might arise, and I was asked to comment on who – if anybody – might be at fault. As I hadn't studied law, I wasn't expected to know the answers – it was presumably to assess my deductive reasoning. As the interview seemed to be coming to a close, the sharp-featured lady unexpectedly shot a question at me, and I was lucky to have internalised my resultant shriek. She asked me whether a confession was ever adequate to convict someone of an offence. At this point, any composure I may have previously clasped to left my body as if water from a colander. I stammered that I didn't believe it was, but didn't really convince myself with the argument that followed. I left the room thinking I'd thrown it all away in the dying minute.'

'The second interview the following day was with a grand old professor in a room which mirrored the first. He was a friendly old stick, and also asked about my accident with almost ghoulish intrigue. I almost managed to bleat on about it for the entire duration of the interview. With ten minutes left to go, he handed me a piece of paper with about six similar but distinct words on it, and asked me to define each and distinguish between them. I cannot remember what the words were, but I do remember thinking that they weren't as complicated as one might expect from an Oxford entrance interview. I may have hesitated a little, thinking this was some kind of trick. But the prof seemed very happy with the distinctions that I made. I left a little baffled by this. It only occurred to me later why I'd been asked this. I guess that it's possible for people to cram a good deal of high concept stuff into their heads before setting off for interview or sitting an exam . . . But that's no good to anyone if they haven't grasped the basics. I suppose the examinations had tested my ability to walk; the professor simply wanted to know if I could crawl.**"**

"I wasn't invited for an interview at any other colleges, and – if I'm honest – left feeling like I'd entirely fluffed my interviews. About a week later, I got an unconditional offer for my first choice college in the post.**"**
OWE CARTER RECENTLY GRADUATED FROM OXFORD WITH A LAW DEGREE

AFTER THE INTERVIEW

Once you're off the premises, make a few notes on the way home. Try to remember who you spoke with, what questions they asked, and how you replied. If you have other interviews coming up, reflect on the experience and consider how you might learn from it and improve your interview technique.

If you weren't happy with one of your answers, don't start beating yourself up about it – interviewers will not reject you on the basis of one answer that wasn't 'perfect'. They will also be taking into account your other answers, your application, your reference and your personal statement, so don't worry too much. If you're really concerned, discuss it with a careers adviser or a tutor.

The next thing you have to do is wait. Keep an eye out for emails and letters concerning offers, invitations for more interviews, or rejections. See Chapter 7 for how to handle any of these, including how to ask for feedback if things didn't go so well.

ADMISSIONS TESTS

It's becoming increasingly common to be asked to supply additional information, or to take tests before, during or after admissions interviews. They vary from course to course and institution to institution, but can take the form of any of the following.

- Sending in copies of recent coursework, such as essays, artwork, projects or reviews
- Writing one or more essays for admissions tutors to support your application
- English language or numeracy tests
- An audition or performance
- A drawing or sketching test
- A critique or questions on an article or passage of text
- Written tests for students from non-standard academic backgrounds
- Questionnaires
- Formal tests
  - BioMedical Admissions Test (BMAT)
  - English Literature Admissions Test (ELAT)
  - Graduate Medical Schools Admissions Test (GAMSAT)
  - History Aptitude Test (HAT)
  - Health Professions Admissions Test (HPAT)
  - Mathematics Aptitude Test (MAT)
  - Modern and Medieval Languages Test (MML)
  - National Admissions Test for Law (LNAT)
  - Physics Aptitude Test (PAT)
  - Sixth Term Examination Papers (STEP)
  - Thinking Skills Assessment, Cambridge (TSA Cambridge)
  - Thinking Skills Assessment, Oxford (TSA Oxford)
  - Thinking Skills Assessment, UCL (TSA)
  - UK Clinical Aptitude Test (UKCAT)

The more competitive or specialist a course, the more likely it is that applicants will be asked to take additional testing. To find out more about which universities and colleges require applicants to provide materials or take tests, see the comprehensive list in *Degree Course Offers* by Brian Heap (published by Trotman), which is updated annually. The author also suggests checking the details with prospectuses, departmental websites and admissions tutors as they are subject to change, and some of them have closing dates. You can also use the *UCAS Big Guide* to check up on admissions tests you might have to take.

❛ If you are asked to sit tests as part of the admissions process, check out uni websites to find out if they have practice tests that you can take before you go. Speak to undergraduates who are already on the course about the test – you could do this on a departmental open day or summer taster courses. If you have specific requirements (such as support for dyslexia) make sure the universities know this so they can make reasonable adjustments accordingly. Look at online practices and preparation tips for medical degree tests (BMAT/UKCAT) and for Law tests (LNAT).**❜**

NAOMI ELFRED, CONNEXIONS PERSONAL ADVISER

Can you do anything to improve your chances of getting a high score? This depends very much upon the type of test, and, if it's a written exam or on-screen test, whether or not you can see past papers (try the websites listed below). With something like drawing or performance, it's a case of practice makes perfect, and trying to relax and project confidence on the day. For subject-specific tests that are knowledge-based, you can take some time to revise the subjects. Assessments for thinking skills and decision-making are harder to prepare for, but you can still try to find past papers, and remember to manage your time carefully during the exam so that you can answer all the questions well and without rushing. Specific test information is listed below.

BioMedical Admissions Test (BMAT)

This is needed for entry to some medical and veterinary schools including the University of Cambridge, Imperial College London, University of Oxford Medical School, Royal Veterinary College, and University College London, and comprises a two-hour paper and pen test administered by Cambridge Assessment. Most candidates sit the BMAT at their own school or college, but others need to use the BMAT Open Centre Network to locate a centre. Applicants must register before the last week of September, and the test is in early November. The EU (including UK) standard entry fee is currently £42.50 and the Rest of the World fee is £72.50. Visit www.admissionstests.cambridgeassessment.org.uk/adt/bmat.

English Literature Admissions Test (ELAT)

This is a 90-minute test, administered by Cambridge Assessment, for entry to undergraduate English courses at the University of Oxford. The test is in essay format, and candidates are required to compare two or three pieces of text. Entries are required by late September, and the test is taken at the start of November. No entry fee. Visit www.admissionstests.cambridgeassessment.org. uk/adt/elat.

Graduate Medical Schools Admissions Test (GAMSAT)

Required for graduate-entry medical or dental schools at: the Peninsula Dental School (4 years); the Peninsula Medical School (5 years undergraduate); the University of Nottingham at Derby (4 years); St George's, University of London (4 years); Swansea University (4 years); and Keele University (4 years). It comprises a five-and-a-half hour test in the third week of September (you must enter by the second week of August), with a fee of £195.00. Results will be available approximately six or seven weeks after the test date. Entry is online via www.gamsatuk.org.

Health Professions Admissions Test (HPAT)

This is needed for study in the Allied Health Professions at the University of Ulster. The relevant courses are: BSc Hons Dietetics, BSc Hons Occupational Therapy, BSc Hons Physiotherapy, BSc Hons Podiatry, BSc Hons Radiography (Diagnostic), BSc Hons Radiography (Therapeutic) and BSc Hons Speech & Language Therapy. Applicants must register by the second week of January, and take the test in the last week of January. It is three hours long, offered at three test centres, and the fee is £95.00. More information and sample questions are available at www.hpat.org.uk.

History Aptitude Test (HAT)

This must be taken by all candidates applying to Oxford for honours degrees in history and its joint schools (Ancient and Modern History, History and Economics, History and English, History and Modern Languages, and History and Politics). The HAT is a two-hour test taken in the first week of November, which requires candidates to read two extracts and answer a total of four questions about them. It is a test of skills, not substantive historical knowledge. Applicants applying through their school need to send a special test declaration form in addition to the

Oxford application form – they take the test at their own school or college. Mature candidates and international candidates will need to contact Oxford University to find out about official centres where they can take the test. www.history.ox.ac.uk/prosundergrad/applying/hat_introduction.htm.

Mathematics Aptitude Test (MAT)

Needed for entry to mathematics or computer science, or a joint honours degree involving mathematics at the University of Oxford. This is a two-and-a-half hour test taken in the first week of November, mainly sat in schools or colleges. Other candidates will need to find a suitable venue by contacting the university: www.ox.ac.uk/admissions/undergraduate_courses/how_to_apply/tests/index.html.

Modern and Medieval Languages Test (MML)

This is needed for entry to modern and medieval languages degrees at the University of Cambridge. The test is taken in the college in which students are being interviewed, while they are in Cambridge for their interview. It takes the format of a 45-minute written test. No fee. Visit www.cam.ac.uk/admissions/undergraduate/courses/mml/tests.html.

National Admissions Test for Law (LNAT)

For entry to a number of law schools: Birmingham, Bristol, Durham, Glasgow, King's College London, Nottingham, Oxford, and University College London. It is a two-and-a-quarter hour computer-based test that includes multiple choice questions and an essay, the date of which is booked during registration. The fee for UK and EU centres is £50.00 (or £70.00 for centres outside the European Union), and the test cannot be revised for, but there are sample questions available free of charge. Entry is via the LNAT website and registration opens at the start of August: www.lnat.ac.uk.

Physics Aptitude Test (PAT)

This is needed for entry to physics, or a joint degree involving physics at the University of Oxford. It is a two-hour test that's taken in the first week of November. Most UK candidates in full-time education are able to take the test at their own schools or colleges, but other candidates should contact the University about test centres and supervisors: www.ox.ac.uk/admissions/undergraduate_courses/how_to_apply/tests/index.html.

Sixth Term Examinations Papers (STEP)

These are compulsory for entry to mathematics at the University of Cambridge and the University of Warwick. Candidates for mathematics at the University of Bristol, the University of Bath, the University of Oxford, and Imperial College London are also encouraged to sit them. They are administered by Cambridge Assessment. The three STEP mathematics papers are sat immediately after A level examinations during the third week of June, and must be taken at a recognised centre. Each paper contains 13 questions and takes three hours to complete. Applications to take STEP should go through a school or college, or go via a recognised test centre. Each paper costs £41.45 to sit. Visit www.admissionstests.cambridgeassessment.org.uk/adt/step.

Thinking Skills Assessment, Cambridge (TSA Cambridge)

This is needed for entry to Computer Science, Economics, Engineering, Land Economy, Natural Sciences (Physical and Biological), and Politics, Psychology and Sociology (PPS) at the University of Cambridge. The TSA is administered during the interview period, and candidates will be informed when they need to take it by the University of Cambridge. It is a multiple-choice test consisting of 50 questions lasting 90 minutes, assessing problem solving and critical thinking. Tests are administered under examination conditions, with an invigilator present. There is no fee. Visit www.admissionstests.cambridgeassessment.org.uk/adt/tsacambridge.

Thinking Skills Assessment, Oxford (TSA Oxford)

Compulsory for anyone applying to study politics & economics (PPE), economics and management (E&M), experimental psychology (EP) or psychology and philosophy at the University of Oxford. A two-hour test that must be applied for by mid-October, and sat in the first week of November. Contains 50 multiple choice questions, and one essay. There is no fee. Visit www.admissionstests. cambridgeassessment.org.uk/adt/tsaoxford.

Thinking Skills Assessment, UCL (TSA)

This must be taken by anyone wishing to take a European Social and Political Studies degree at University College London (UCL). It is a 90-minute test, containing 50 multiple choice questions. The test is arranged by UCL when you apply and is normally taken while you are in London for your interview. There is no fee. Visit www.admissionstests.cambridgeassessment.org.uk/adt/tsaucl.

UK Clinical Aptitude Test (UKCAT)

Required for entry to the majority of medical and dental schools. Registration is online, via www.ukcat.ac.uk, with an entry deadline of the third week of September. Tests are computer-based, last two hours, begin in the middle of June, and run through to the first or second week of October. If you sit the test between early July and end-August the test fee is £60.00 for EU entrants and £95.00 for non-EU entrants. If you sit the test between early September and the second week of October the test fee is £75.00 EU, and £95.00 non-EU.

I recently sat the MAT as part of my application to study mathematics at Hertford College at the University of Oxford. It was absolutely terrifying! Two of us sat the paper at our local college, and we were outnumbered by the invigilators. You get two and a half hours to complete it and there are five main questions, each split up into several other smaller questions. The first part was multiple-choice questions, where you get four marks for each correct answer, and no marks for showing your workings. They give you about a third of a sheet of A4 to do your workings for each one. The remaining four questions are written questions and you have about 20 minutes per question, and your workings-out are counted. It's a very difficult exam, and I felt woefully under-prepared. It's true that the questions are based on subjects that you'd find on the AS level syllabus, but it felt very different in its presentation. You need to show evidence of very high levels of application of your knowledge, perhaps something you might find in the second or third year of most university mathematics courses. Scary.

You are not sent the results of the exam; you get an invitation for an interview at Oxford, or not. I didn't get into Oxford but I have no regrets: it was worth doing. It's quite a valuable insight to what you would be doing at degree level. My advice would be to treat it with the same importance as an A level exam, and prepare for it months in advance. Find as many past papers as you can from their website and practice. Don't just rely on reading your AS syllabus as it won't be enough. However smart you think you are, don't think you can just turn up and be OK. Go to their website and find out everything you can beforehand. **,**

MARK C. MUNRO, AGE 23

SUMMARY:
TOP TIPS FOR INTERVIEWS AND TESTS

1. Think like an interviewer. They want to see a positive attitude, a pleasant personality, concentration, and independent, critical and analytical thought.

2. Know when interviews take place. Check the information for all of the courses you have applied for to see if and when they are likely to hold interviews. Make sure you are available during this period in case you're invited.

3. Confirm and understand. Reply to invitations from universities and colleges in a timely fashion. Make a note of dates and times in your diary. Find out how long the interviews are, how many there will be, and whether it's a panel, group or informal interview.

4. Preparation pays off. Practical details such as arranging travel, location, and interview outfits can help you to look and feel organised and confident. Practice interviews, reading the papers, looking up possible careers, and re-reading the prospectus, all help you increase your knowledge and reduce nervousness.

5. Anticipate questions. Think about the most common interview questions and come up with some convincing answers beforehand.

Just make sure it doesn't sound too rehearsed. Re-read your personal statement before setting off too, as many interviewers base questions on this.

6. Sometimes there is no right answer. Some interview questions are deliberately designed to see how you approach problems and work them through, or apply existing knowledge to completely new situations. Getting 'the perfect answer' is less important than your process.

7. Take 'informal' seriously. It's still an interview and you can win or lose a place on the strength of it. Failure to attend an informal interview can result in an offer being withdrawn.

8. 'Look' smart on the telephone. Even if you're not there in person, you need to be organised and make a good general impression to do well in a telephone interview.

9. Put tests in the diary. If you have to complete a formal test as part of your application, make sure you know the deadlines for registering and taking the test, and for obtaining the results.

10. Test-run your tests. Many tests cannot be studied for in terms of factual knowledge, but it can be a great help to try some sample papers beforehand as it helps you with thinking skills and timing, and may calm your nerves.

CHAPTER SEVEN
OFFERS, REJECTIONS AND UCAS EXTRA

In the last chapter we looked at the ins and outs of the interview process and other university invitations, and now we turn to the final decisions: different types of offers, rejections, and how to handle them. If you applied via UCAS and aren't holding any offers at the end of the decisions period, you can then opt to go through UCAS Extra if you want to.

UCAS OFFERS AND REJECTIONS

Most students apply through UCAS, and they are contacted about decisions via UCAS's online Track service. To use Track, all that's needed is your personal ID number, and your Track username and password. If you've lost your password, contact the UCAS Customer Service Unit.

Some universities and colleges will send you an acknowledgement to let you know that your offer has arrived and they are considering it, but others do not send any messages at all until they've made their decisions.

Deadlines for university replies

- Ideally, universities are supposed to send UCAS their decisions before the end of March, provided your applications to them were made before the cut-off point of mid-January.
- It can be very difficult sitting back and waiting to hear from them, but it's better not to keep phoning institutions up and bothering them – they don't have to reply before their absolute deadline in early May (6th of May in 2011).
- Nagging can sometimes backfire, so keep your cool at least until the end of March.

' I really REALLY want to know if I've got into Dundee: my heart is actually set on it. I keep checking my UCAS Track three times a day to see if they have said anything but there's nothing so far. My Nan said to me, "A watched kettle never boils," and she's right. I need to find something really exciting to do to take my mind off it but nothing is working so far. No matter how many times they tell you, "Every uni gets back at different times, don't worry if yours takes a while," it never helps. **'**

KYLE MEARS, AGE 17, RUNSHAW COLLEGE

☑ TIP

If you get offers to join your top one or two favourite courses, you can make your acceptances without having to wait until all the other decisions have arrived.

There are only three standard possibilities that will show up on Track when universities reply to you:

1 **A conditional offer:** you are offered a place provided you meet certain conditions. This usually means that you must gain certain grades in particular exam subjects, or attain a minimum number of tariff points. You might also be asked to gain certain grades in individual units that are part of your exam subjects. In most cases, you will be asked to meet the conditions of your offer by the end of August (unless you're taking winter exams).

2 **An unconditional offer:** you are offered a place and do not have to meet any other conditions. This either happens because they really like you, or because you've already sat your exams before applying and your grades or equivalent experience were good enough. Check the small print though, as a few courses will ask you for payments upfront, or medical checks before you can start your studies.

3 **An 'unsuccessful application':** you are rejected by whoever you've applied to. They are not legally obliged to explain their reasons for rejecting you, but they may tell you via Track.

Whenever new offers and rejections are made via UCAS, you should receive an email notifying you of changes to your Track. If you didn't supply an email address, these will arrive as letters in the post instead. You may also be sent a letter or email directly from a university or college, but the decision is not official until you've been notified by UCAS themselves.

☑ **TIP**

Make sure that you've added UCAS to your 'safe senders' email list, and log in from time to time to make sure you aren't missing anything.

To view an offer after a notification, go to your Choices page in Track and click on the course code for that choice. You should then be able to view any conditions that might have been laid down in the offer, plus any other information that the university has sent along with it.

☑ **TIP**

Occasionally, offers are withdrawn by a college or university. If this happens they are obliged to explain the reason that they changed their minds, and this will show up on Track. For example, it can happen if students decline the opportunity to attend an informal interview, or fail to reply to their emails or letters.

'I'm still waiting on all my offers. I thought I got one the other day but it was actually sent in error from the university. That was a bit disappointing but I am sure I will hear something soon though.'
ANONYMOUS STUDENT, AGE 18

Different types of conditional offer

A university or college might make you a 'joint conditional offer'. For example, after applying to one course you may be offered a place on a degree or an HND, with the university or college deciding which type of course to put you on after they've seen your examination results. In this instance if you accept the offer you are accepting the whole offer – be careful you are not accepting a potential place on an HND if you are certain that you don't want to study for one.

Sometimes, universities and colleges offer applicants places on courses that they haven't applied to. They tend to be similar to the original choice, but can be in a different format, require lower grades, or include a conversion course or year's foundation. If this happens to you, check with the institution that they meant to make you this offer, and if that's correct, ask them to explain why. Do not accept an offer of this nature unless you have thoroughly read through the course details, have had an opportunity to discuss it with admissions staff, understand the financial implications, and are satisfied that it meets your requirements and standards.

Responding to your offers

If all your institutions have told UCAS whether they're going to make you an offer or reject your application, and you have been made at least one offer, UCAS will then email you and ask you to reply to your offers:

- If you receive decisions from all your choices before the end of March, UCAS usually asks you to respond to them by the first week of May. Your exact deadline will be included in the email they send you.
- If you receive decisions from all your choices before the first week of May, UCAS usually asks you to respond to them by the first week of June. Again, your exact deadline will be included in the email they send you.
- If you do not reply to an offer by the date you are given, UCAS will automatically decline all the offers you are holding.

If you have a question about a decision, contact the university or college for more advice. Take some time to review and reflect upon your choices and options before you finally decide to accept an offer of a place on a course – higher education is a big commitment and you will be spending the next few years in it.

You reply to any offers you have been made by using Track, once you're sure that you've completely made up your mind.

Responding to conditional offers

Conditional offers are usually based on your exam results. If you accept a conditional offer you must meet the requirements by the end of August that year, even if you are applying for deferred entry the following year. If you're sitting winter exams, this date may be even earlier. If you've been made a conditional offer, when you've sat your exams the results of A and AS levels will be sent directly to the institutions you've chosen.

Your possible responses to conditional offers depend on how you feel about them, and what other types of offer you've received. Your options include:

- conditional firm choice (CF)
- conditional insurance choice (CI)
- decline the offer.

If you receive one conditional offer and the remainder of the decisions are rejections, and you decide to take the offer, you use Track to make a conditional firm acceptance (CF). You must then meet the conditions of acceptance to gain a place on the course. Once you have met the conditions, your decision is binding and you have to take up this place.

If you receive more than one conditional offer, you may pick a conditional insurance choice (CI) as well as a firm choice if you wish. Most people who make an insurance choice of this type go for an offer where the grades or points are slightly lower, just in case they don't do as well as they'd hoped in their exams. If you miss your target for the firm choice, but meet the conditions for the insurance choice, your decision is binding and you will be expected to attend your insurance course.

☑ TIP

You don't have to make an insurance choice if you don't want to, so don't make an insurance acceptance unless you're completely certain you'd be happy to study that course.

Responding to unconditional offers

Your possible options here include:

- unconditional firm choice (UF)
- unconditional insurance choice (UI)
- decline the offer.

If you are made an unconditional offer, and it's the course you most want to do out of all your available options, you should make an unconditional firm acceptance (UF). You must then decline all other offers, as you've fully committed to attending this course. There's no need to pick an insurance choice. Congratulations, you're going into higher education!

You may find yourself in a situation where you hold both conditional and unconditional offers, but your first choice is conditional and your second choice is unconditional. If that's the case, you can make a firm conditional acceptance (CF) of your first choice, and an unconditional insurance acceptance of your second (UI) choice. Again, if you fail to meet the conditions of your first choice, you are bound by the rules of UCAS to attend your second choice course, so don't make that unconditional insurance acceptance if you're not 100% sure about it.

HIGH FLYERS, NO OFFERS

After exceptionally high numbers of applications last year, many A level students with very high predicted grades and generally impressive CVs found themselves with no offers after making their applications. Most of these applicants had applied for popular, prestigious courses and were confident they'd be able to meet the entry requirements and average offers of the colleges and universities that they'd applied to. What can you do if you find yourself in this situation? The most important thing is not to panic, as there are still many avenues open to you. You can:

- search for other course places through Extra (see Chapter 7)
- seek out careers advice to decide whether you still want to study that subject, or whether you'd like to follow the same career. You may wish to consider other related subjects or related careers, or try something completely different (see Chapter 1 for resources)
- concentrate on getting the best A level results you possibly can to back up future applications
- look for places through Clearing (Chapter 8), as all kinds of places may become available at this time

- reapply for the following year's university intake for the same subject, or different subjects, by which time you will already have your A level grades
- use the year out to take extra exams, gain relevant work experience, and undertake other relevant extra-curricular activities to add to your second application
- apply to study abroad at top universities such as Harvard in the United States (see page 57 for where to start if you're thinking about overseas study).

' You might be feeling quite worried in this situation, especially if your other friends have their options sorted out, but try not to feel too pressured as there are options out there. The main thing is that you choose the right option for you, rather than picking something you feel you won't enjoy. It's good to seek support and ask for more advice at this stage. '
STACEY CARTER, CONNEXIONS PERSONAL ADVISER

Getting a full set of rejections, or changing your mind

You may find yourself in a situation where you are rejected by all of the institutions you've applied to. If this happens, check to see whether you fulfil the requirements for the chance to find a different place through UCAS Extra (page 143) or the Clearing process (Chapter 8). You also have a number of other options, including reapplying the following year, re-sitting exams, taking a gap year, or applying for jobs.

' If you change your mind about your studies at the point where you're already being made offers by universities and colleges, the first port of call is to speak to a Personal/ Careers Adviser regarding your decision-making processes and analysis. Why the change? What triggered it? And so on.

Then if you definitely do want to study something else, phone the university, explain your reasons and ask about transferring. If you are a good candidate and there are spaces on the new course it might be possible. Secondly, you could reject your offers and go through UCAS Extra or Clearing. This is a risky approach but it is an option. The third step is to take a gap year, reflect on it and re-apply. **》**

NIKKI BRUNNING, CONNEXIONS PERSONAL ADVISER

For a number of reasons, including changes in personal circumstances, students sometimes decide to decline all of the offers they are holding. In this case, they are normally eligible to use UCAS Extra or Clearing if they wish.

Other students may decide to withdraw from the UCAS application scheme altogether. This is easily done by submitting their decision via Track. Once they have done this, they are not allowed to go through Extra or Clearing, and should they still wish to enter higher education they will have to complete a fresh application the following year.

Oxford and Cambridge

There can be a slightly different format to degree course offers from Oxford and Cambridge. If you are successful you may be given a place on your chosen course at your favourite college. These conditional and unconditional offers are made via UCAS, and you respond to them in the standard way.

At Cambridge you may also be placed in a 'pool' – which means that you haven't been necessarily given a place at your first choice of college, but you might still get into Cambridge. If your Cambridge application is pooled, you may be:

- asked to attend a further interview in early January at another college (allowing for AS/A level module assessments held during this time)
- offered a place at another college without a further interview
- contacted by the college you applied to/were allocated to, normally by the end of January, if no college is able to offer you a place.

Around one in five applicants are pooled, and around one in four pooled applicants receives an offer of a place.

NON-UCAS OFFERS AND REJECTIONS

If you've applied directly to universities, colleges or other institutions for entry onto certain courses, they will contact you directly with their decisions, usually in writing or sometimes by email. You are likely to be asked to reply in writing to accept or decline, or to return an enclosed reply slip stating your intentions. If you accept a conditional offer and have met all the conditions to win a place on the course, you'll be the person responsible for sending proof of your results to the admissions office as soon as you have them. You may then be asked to fill in extra paperwork to confirm your final acceptance of the place.

Other application routes

CUKAS and GTTR applications (see Chapter 4) are made online, and their offers and replies system is based on UCAS Track. You can find out more about responding to offers here: www.cukas.ac.uk or www.gttr.ac.uk.

WHAT HAPPENS AFTER YOU ACCEPT AN OFFER AND FULFIL ALL CONDITIONS?

Once you've completely committed to a course, and have met all of the conditions that the university or college have asked for, UCAS will send you their confirmation letter in the post.

Your chosen institution will also begin sending you information to help you get ready for your first term. This will include accommodation details, and other information about arrival, induction, enrolment, payment of fees, and so on. There will also be subject-specific information, perhaps including a reading list, and additional documentation may be required for certain courses (e.g. Criminal Records Bureau forms, required vaccinations or other medical clearance). If you haven't done so already, now is the time to apply for funding, course-specific bursaries and so on.

DEALING WITH REJECTION

Not everyone gets offered the place of their dreams. Universities and colleges turn students down for a variety of reasons, such as:

- too many applicants for the course (quite simply you can't all get in, no matter how good your grades or interview skills are)
- the course was already full by the time you applied
- not meeting the entry requirements (predicted grades too low etc.)
- a badly-written application, containing mistakes or inaccuracies
- lack of awareness of what the course entails
- lack of knowledge about what a related career or vocation involves
- not looking interested or committed enough
- appearing arrogant or smug on the application or at the interview
- poor performance at interview: extreme nervousness or shyness, immaturity, inability to understand questions and give intelligent answers, being rude or unfriendly.

Rejection unfortunately is part of life. Try not to dwell on it but reflect on why, and then move on. If all your universities have rejected you try to turn this into a positive. Don't panic as there are other options, including UCAS Extra, Clearing, a gap year, a job to make some cash, or maybe a rethink and going into employment with training or apprenticeships etc. You could always go to university later (and hopefully richer!) as a mature student, but the downside is that sometimes you have other responsibilities by then.

FRASER SHADWELL, CONNEXIONS PERSONAL ADVISER

Being rejected is never easy, particularly if you're rejected by your first choice, and sometimes it comes as a shock. There are often strong feelings of disappointment, anger or loss, and it's better to get them out of your system constructively rather than bottling things up or pretending you aren't upset. Cry, punch a cushion, talk it out with a sympathetic friend or relative: whatever it takes. If things aren't going to plan then you still need to try to make the best of the situation and develop new priorities and strategies, preferably with help from a careers or higher education adviser. Then you have to move on to the next task, and hopefully learn something constructive from the experience.

Although you might be feeling a bit sensitive at this point, you have to reflect upon how things have gone and that means being brutally honest with yourself.

Look through the common reasons for rejection listed above – do any of them apply to you? Think about your choices …

- If you applied for a highly popular course that's incredibly competitive, and you genuinely think you did all the right things to get in, it might simply be that it was oversubscribed and they couldn't offer you a place.
- Could you have applied earlier, before all the places were filled? Can you wait to apply again next year or should you move on to something different?
- Go back and check the entry requirements for everything you've applied for, and be certain that you've met all of them.
- Are your predicted grades too low for what you wanted to do? It's OK to try your luck with one or two courses, but not with all your choices. If you truly think your actual grades will be much better than your predicted ones, would you be better off applying after taking your exams?
- Do you really know enough about the university or college, the course, and where the subject might take your future career?
- Are you being honest with yourself about your real areas of interest and talent? For example, have you been pushed into something by peer or parental pressure that really isn't the best subject for you?
- Get your application and personal statement checked again. Is it really showing you off at your best? Have you been too modest?
- If possible, look at your reference: could it be holding you back somehow?
- Think back through any interviews that you'd had, and consider what might not have gone so well. If you have any more interviews arranged, how can you improve your performance?

If you have a reasonable idea of what went wrong, you can then make the necessary changes to improve your chances of future success. Don't be scared to take a little time out to give matters some more thought. On the other hand, you might be mystified about being unsuccessful with a particular application, in which case you might want to write to the college or university in question to ask for some detailed feedback. Institutions are not obliged to give you any further information after rejecting you, but asking politely can work wonders. Their reply might be a tough read, but be prepared for that and ultimately you might find the whole exercise is very useful in the long run.

Occasionally applicants are mistakenly sent a rejection message when admissions tutors meant to make them an offer. Also, in a few cases information has gone missing from application forms, and applicants have been rejected because they appeared to be under-qualified. These errors were picked up because potential students sent polite emails to their university or college of choice to query the decisions they'd received. You can also appeal against a decision, by saying to admissions staff that you're disappointed, and that you're still very keen to join the course in question if there are any places left. This is not guaranteed to work, especially if it's a very popular course that attracts highly qualified candidates, but it has worked for some people.

Sylvia Zalk, Programme Officer at Imperial College, London has some wise words about understanding the reasons behind a rejection, and has helpful tips for responding to it in the most positive manner:

The rejection process is pretty swift and painless. It's usually just down to competitiveness, as Imperial is very popular and we can ask for a high standard of student, which we normally seem to get. That's the standard rejection blurb. If a student is persistent we'll pull out their file and try and give them more info. Lack of demonstrable enthusiasm is a really big one, as enthusiasm often triumphs over so-so qualifications. A very qualified student who takes a blasé attitude probably won't get in. In fact any sort of arrogance is best avoided. As an example we ask all students to complete an aptitude test. Some can't be bothered and think that sending a URL to one of their sites will do, but it won't. Poor English is another one, regardless of whether or not they have the required TOEFL score. The course leader normally decides who to reject, however sometimes a form arrives from Registry with a

"Not eligible" sticker on it, which we just need to sign off. We usually send rejections through to Registry, and let them do the dirty work! The students find out online.**,**

....

' A student should react by accepting the rejection, and asking how they can improve so that they can get in next year. Asking about possible work experience they can gain in the meantime is good. We have about 120 applicants for 40 places, and the course leaders tend to remember the people who apply, so if they see that you've taken their advice seriously and are really keen you could get an offer. Students shouldn't send their mums in to quibble the rejection, as happened to me the other day. Neither should students bother to appeal, as that NEVER works! **,**

UCAS EXTRA

The UCAS Extra service opens at the end of February, and allows UCAS applicants who are not holding any offers to apply for courses with vacancies. Last year, 5,619 students were accepted onto university or college courses via Extra. Only one course can be applied for at a time, and Extra closes at the start of July. In 2011 the start date is the 25th of February, and the last possible date for making an Extra application is the 6th of July.

To be eligible for Extra you must have:

- already used up all of your original five course choices, AND
- have had answers from all the institutions you applied to, AND
- have either had no offers or declined all offers (this includes failing to reply before your deadline and being declined by default).

For a variety of reasons, applicants may sometimes decide that they want to decline any offers they've been made, so they can try their luck with other courses and institutions through Extra or Clearing. If that includes you, think hard about the decision and don't make it in a hurry. Do as much research as possible and take plenty of advice. It's vital to realise that once you've declined those offers and entered into the Extra process, there's no going back to your original choices – the decision to decline them is final and irreversible.

> ❛ It IS possible to find good places in Extra. People don't have to pick their firm/insurance choices before May at the earliest, and Extra opens at the end of February, so "popular" universities may have courses in Extra, but in general they will be the less competitive ones (e.g. maths or languages rather than history or English). The reason courses are put into Extra is because the institutions concerned reckon that they can continue to make offers for the time being, given what they know about patterns of acceptance of the offers they have already made by then, and the numbers who might actually achieve their offer conditions in August. That said, the number of courses in Extra might be rather lower this round than previously, because of the generally higher number of applicants this year and the increased pressure on places across the board, not just at the "top" universities. ❜
>
> **GEORGE PRICE, CAREERS ADVICE SERVICE OFFICER, MANCHESTER**

How to apply via Extra

You can use the Extra service online via UCAS's Track facility. Log onto Track on the first day that you're eligible to start using Extra (last week of February) and you'll see a button marked 'Extra' has appeared. Simply click on the button to get started, and UCAS will forward your application to the new university or college of your choice.

The easiest way to find course vacancies is by looking through UCAS's 'Course Search' function (www.ucas.com). If there are still places on any courses, they will have an 'X' marked next to them. It's also a very good idea to contact favourite universities or colleges directly to see what they currently have available – this will allow you to ask important questions, build up a rapport with admissions staff, and make sure that you are eligible to apply.

If you applied for extremely competitive courses, or popular and selective universities, and didn't get in the first time around, you need to think hard about the alternatives (if you haven't already done so). Seek advice on your options from your school or college's higher education adviser, or a careers adviser, before making your mind up.

☑ **TIP**

Don't start applying through Extra until you fully understand how this system works. You can only apply for one course at a time, so you need to make your decisions and do your research carefully.

It's essential to do as much research as possible before you apply to a new course. Take the time to go back and follow the main tips in Chapter 1 and Chapter 2 of this book to help you to decide on the right course and the right university or college for you. The latest edition of *Degree Course Offers* by Brian Heap (published by Trotman) can also give you plenty of useful information. If time allows, try to visit the institution in person or talk things through with someone at the admissions office before deciding. Once you've made your mind up, the Course Search entry profiles on the UCAS website will give you some handy tips about making your application.

As you can only apply to one institution at a time, it makes sense to go straight for your new first choice. This can be:

- a similar subject to your original choices but in a different location
- a new subject with one of your original first choice institutions, or
- a radically different course in a new location.

The choice is yours, but remember that during the Extra process UCAS will still have to forward your original personal statement and reference. This can cause some very awkward questions to be raised by admissions tutors about your commitment to a subject if it greatly differs from your first round of applications, but you may be able to get around the problem by writing a new personal statement and forwarding it directly to the admissions tutors for the new course, so check with them first. You'll also have to ask your referee to create a new reference.

> I have just applied through Extra for an entirely different course. I originally applied to do midwifery and was unsuccessful from all my choices. This made me sit down and have a long hard think about whether it was actually what I wanted to do, and I came to the conclusion that it was not. I have now applied for a degree in animal management. I'm very apprehensive about the whole thing, the entire process of applying to university is horrible and it really did knock my confidence a lot getting rejected from five places.

> I think now though I'm a bit more positive as I know that this new course is something that I would love to do and hopefully be good at. I am really grateful that I have had the opportunity to apply for it this year, and even if I don't get in at least I was able to try. I'm now addicted to checking Track again already! But hopefully I will hear soon so I don't work myself up too much like before.

CARLY HORWOOD, AGE 17

UCAS Extra decisions

Once your application has been forwarded by UCAS, the university or college has 21 days to consider your application:

- The university may make you an unconditional or conditional offer. If you accept either type of offer you become committed to the course, which means that you are no longer eligible to make any more applications through Extra. In other words, it counts as a firm choice when you accept, just like the standard UCAS application. Should you fail to meet the requirements for an accepted conditional offer when the exam results come out, you then become eligible for Clearing.

- Don't leap blindly at the first offer you receive. Only accept the offer of a place if you are 100% sure that you want to take this particular course at this particular college or university. After all, you're committing to at least three years of your time, and that's before you even think about funding. Do not make a rushed or panic decision.

- If the institution makes you an offer and you decide to reject the offer, you can apply for other courses (one at a time) if you have enough time remaining. Remember that Extra finishes at the start of July.

- If the college or university sends you a rejection, your Extra button will quickly be reactivated in Track and you can apply straight away to another institution, provided there's enough time. Contact the new course's admissions staff to double check the availability of places, and its suitability.

- Every 21 days the Track system gives you the opportunity to apply elsewhere if you're waiting for a decision and have changed your mind about the institution you're currently waiting to hear from. It's best to contact the college or university first to discuss things with them before you apply somewhere different.

- If you only receive rejections, or if you decide to decline all offers during the Extra period, you will then have to wait for your exam results. At that point you will automatically become eligible for Clearing (see Chapter 8 for full details).

📋 SUMMARY: OFFERS, REJECTIONS AND UCAS EXTRA

1. Check your deadlines. If you don't reply to offers before the individual deadline you've been given, UCAS will automatically decline all your offers and you'll lose them.

2. Be patient. The universities and colleges have longer to reply to applicants than you might realise, so don't start nagging them too soon – it creates a bad impression.

3. Understand how to accept. Provided you get at least two offers, you have a number of choices open to you if you decide to make one or more acceptances. Be careful with those replies!

4. Like your insurance. Only accept a course offer as an insurance choice if you're completely happy to study there. It's a binding agreement, and while you can get out of it, this process can take a long time.

5. Get feedback on rejections. Universities and colleges are not obliged to tell you why your application was unsuccessful, but if asked politely, their feedback can often be very useful and constructive, and help you to ensure future success.

6. Nobody likes rejection. Acknowledge it if you're really feeling upset, and talk things through with a sympathetic person to get it out of your system. Then you can move on to take some positive action.

7. Query anything unusual. University staff are only human and occasionally make mistakes, and sometimes software and computer systems can act strangely. If you're confused or surprised by an offer or a rejection, contact the higher education institution.

8. Should you appeal? Provided you are very polite and enthusiastic, you have nothing to lose if you decide to appeal following an unsuccessful application. The worst they can do is say no.

9. Think before you cancel. If you completely withdraw your UCAS application, you will be unable to use their Extra or Clearing services. Simply declining all your offers will not have this effect.

10. Make an Extra attempt. If you haven't found a place so far, the Extra system allows you to apply to one new course at a time, provided they have spaces and you meet the entry conditions. If it doesn't work out then you automatically become eligible to use Clearing.

CHAPTER EIGHT
CLEARING AND ADJUSTMENT

Unless you've accepted an unconditional offer by this stage of the process, you will probably be waiting for your A level results to be published in August. Sometimes things don't go according to plan and you may find that you've performed less well, or much better, than you'd hoped. At this time of year universities may have unfilled places left on some of the courses that they teach (often because applicants' exam results didn't meet their offers) and you could be sent a 'changed offer', or become eligible to use the Clearing or Adjustment processes.

AFTER A LEVEL RESULTS ARE PUBLISHED

It is always advisable to be available on the morning when A level results come out (unless you've already accepted an unconditional offer). If you're holding any conditional offers, on that day you will find out whether you have met them, exceeded them, or failed to meet them. Alternatively, you may not be holding any offers. At this point, a number of possibilities may open up, and you can follow them in Track.

- If you've met your conditional offer, you will be accepted by your firm choice. You will then be sent a letter confirming your place.
- If you've met and exceeded your conditional offer, you can still go to your firm choice of institution if you wish, or you may wish to rethink your options and perhaps opt to use the Adjustment process (see page 168) as part of this.
- If you have just missed your grades, the situation becomes complicated. You might still be accepted by your firm choice, or you could be given a 'changed offer' notice where you're offered a place on a different course. Research changed offers very carefully and don't

feel obliged to accept them if you don't think they're right for you. You might also be rejected by your first choice.

- If you have missed your grades by a wider margin and been rejected by your firm choice, or if you are holding no offers at this stage you become eligible for Clearing.

' My offer was BBC, but on Results Day I got ABD. I thought my firm choice would be lenient as I'd only missed my offer by one grade. They took two days to update Track after the results came out to tell me I'd been rejected from my original choice (Speech and Language Therapy) and been offered a place on their almost empty Health Studies course, which was too general and non-vocational and I didn't want it. I had already been rejected from my insurance choice so that was my only offer. Because the university had taken so long to get back to me, Clearing had already been open for two days, and as a result I missed out on places on any other Speech and Language Therapy course (apart from ones that informed me that they could put me on the reserve list, but I'd be about 10th in line). '

' My advice? Even if you are certain that you will meet your offer, be prepared not to. About a week before your results come out, research a good selection of universities that offer your course and make a note of their Clearing telephone number. If your firm and insurance choices don't get back to you by midday on results day, ring them up (preferably not their Clearing number, as this can get busy) and ask what your application status is. If they are still undecided about whether to accept you, it may be best to ask them to release you, so that you have time to find a good place through Clearing. **,**

FIONA KIDD, AGE 19, RECEIVED AN UNCONDITIONAL OFFER AFTER REAPPLYING

ABOUT THE CLEARING PROCESS

'Clearing' is a service run by UCAS for people who haven't already secured a place at a university or college during the current year. The process allows students to apply for the empty places that are still available. It starts on the same day that A level results come out (in early August in Scotland and mid August for the rest of the UK) and runs until the third week of October, although most activity takes place during August.

DATES FOR CLEARING IN 2011

- Clearing begins on the 4th of August in Scotland and on 18th of August in the rest of the UK.
- The 30th of September is the date that the Clearing vacancy search closes.
- The 24th of October is the last date to add a Clearing choice in UCAS Track, and the last date institutions can accept any Clearing applicants.

Clearing could be described as 'the final round' of the UCAS admissions cycle, and it's effectively your last chance to find a university place for the current academic year.

Every year approximately 100,000 students find themselves eligible for Clearing, although many of them decide to go straight into the world of work, or to wait and reapply for courses the following year. If you decide to go through the Clearing process you'll be in good company: over 47,000 students gained a university place during Clearing last year, so they made up just under 10% of all first year undergraduates.

Many students are mystified by the Clearing process, but it's actually fairly straightforward once you get started, as we're about to see.

Darren Barker from UCAS

‚ The UCAS Clearing process is here to help students if they haven't received the grades that they were expecting. Clearing is a structured and well-organised service, backed by a knowledgeable team of advisers whose experience and understanding make the process simple to use. Going through Clearing doesn't mean in any way that a student has failed. They may have had offers from a university or college that they didn't meet; it simply might be that they applied late; or, they may decide that they don't actually want to go to their first choice university any more. ‚

You could begin to do some Clearing research long before the A level results come out, to give you a headstart just in case things don't go so well. Go back over your original applications and personal statement, think about your choices, and find out about alternative courses and locations that you might be interested in that accept slightly lower grades.

‚ I was unsuccessful at all four of my choices for grad-entry medicine, and I had no idea medicine places could appear in Clearing. Late in August I got a call from Warwick saying some places had opened up, but I would have to make a decision either way in 24 hours and there was no opportunity to defer. It was simple to do on the website – I received an unconditional offer on Track, accepted it by calling UCAS and sent off my information to Warwick. I was really apprehensive at having to leave home because I had counted on taking a year out, and all of a sudden I had to pack bags and make new plans! I'm very glad it all worked out. ‚

MARCUS, AGED 22

☑ TIP

Check the UCAS Exam Results page (www.ucas.com) to see the list of qualifications that they receive from different exam boards. If your qualification is not listed, YOU are responsible for informing your chosen college or university about your results.

Done better than expected?

Around 40% of predicted grades are wrong, and some lucky students get much better grades than they were hoping for. If you are one of these lucky people, and you're already holding an offer of a place from a university or college, you might decide to try for a place on a different course. There's a new way to do this without risking the offer that you already hold – turn to page 168 to find out more about Adjustment.

WHO IS ELIGIBLE TO APPLY THROUGH CLEARING?

You are eligible to use Clearing if you have applied through UCAS for a university place in the current application year (and have not withdrawn your application), and if you meet any of the following criteria:

- you hold no offers
- your conditional offers have not been confirmed because you didn't meet the conditions (usually this is because you didn't get high enough grades)
- you have declined any offers you were given, or you have failed to confirm your offers in time before the cut-off date
- your offers have not been confirmed and you have also declined any alternative offers from the same university
- you have applied after the end of June deadline, which is the 30th of June in 2011, so UCAS was unable to forward your application.

☑ TIP

To use Clearing, you must have paid the full UCAS application fee of £21. If you only applied for one course and paid just £11 to begin with, and your application was declined or unsuccessful, you will then need to pay the extra £10.

UCAS's Darren Barker says that: 'UCAS is the only way that applicants can enter Clearing, because they would have to have applied through UCAS in order to get a Clearing number if they become eligible. This number is required by the institutions who are offering places over the Clearing period. The Clearing number can be found on Track, the system used by applicants to check the progress of their UCAS application.'

HOW DOES THE CLEARING PROCESS WORK?

1. A level results are published
2. Check you qualify for Clearing
3. Get your Clearing number
4. Research available degree courses
5. Contact universities and colleges
6. Institution(s) may provisionally offer you a place
7. You accept by adding one Clearing choice to UCAS Track
8. University formally accepts you via Track
9. UCAS officially confirms your place by writing to you

Darren Barker warns: 'It would be wise not to book any holidays at this time of year. If you don't get the grades that you were looking for, you need to be available over the Clearing period to speak to institutions that you are interested in and ask them questions about the course. You will have to be around in person to answer questions and make important decisions. It is worth noting that many of the popular courses are snapped up quickly on the first day of Clearing. The early bird catches the worm!'

❝ On A level results day, some of the students who don't get their predicted grades phone us feeling distressed. We listen to these students, empathise and give personal examples. We challenge their perception that their life has been ruined. We encourage seeing the bigger picture and help them understand there are other options that may also help. Emotions are strong feelings and will pass. It is normal to feel like this. *

*Students receive practical support from us as well. They should phone the university as they may still have places and still be willing to accept them. UCAS Clearing, taking a gap year, and reapplying are also possible solutions. It is also important that they understand why entrance grades have been set and that they relate to being able to cope with the level of study, so, for some students, post-18 employment is more appropriate. *

NAOMI ELFRED, CONNEXIONS PERSONAL ADVISER

DEALING WITH THE STRESS AND FALLOUT

If you got lower grades than you were expecting, it's quite normal to feel crushed, miserable, anxious or stressed out. If you need to, then go off and have a cry and let it all out. Get some support from a sympathetic friend or relative as well if that's helpful. Then it's time to take a deep breath and start to take action.

Before you think about Clearing, contact your first choice university to see whether they'll still be happy to take you. If you only slipped a grade or two, made a good impression at interview, or there have been personal circumstances such as illness or bereavement, some universities will still admit you onto your chosen course. If this fails, you may still be offered an alternative place on one of their other courses. You should also contact the institution that offered you an insurance place.

If nothing suitable comes up, although you might be feeling stressed, do not despair. Your life has not been ruined and all is not lost, in spite of what you might think. Plenty of options remain available at this point. If you have reasonable exam results then there's still a very good chance that you will find yourself another place. Although this new course might not initially have been your first choice, you may find it suits you very well and it could even be more enjoyable than your original one.

Picking a course and location

When you get your results, and you find that you're eligible for Clearing, take a few moments to work out what you want to do. If you do decide you want to enter Clearing, get enough information together before you start. Go back over what you've already learned about courses that would suit you, and consider your career aspirations and subject choices. Talk possible options through with your careers adviser at college, your other tutors or a Connexions adviser (080 800 13 2 19). Think carefully about subject, location and course format, financial and other factors, and rank them roughly in order of personal importance

- **Subject.** With Clearing you are not limited to the subjects that you originally applied for, so if you've had a change of heart you are free to research and act upon it. However, you may wish to try for similar courses in different locations, or slightly different courses at the original locations (for example, if you didn't get in to study medicine, you might consider a biomedical sciences degree instead). Look for course content, class sizes, and teaching scores. Don't accept a place on a course you don't really want at your favourite university in the hope of transferring to your ideal course later – this simply isn't possible at many institutions.
- **Location.** Think about distance from home, campus or city universities, academic and other facilities and the social scene.
- **Format.** You may wish to consider courses with different formats, such as sandwich degrees (where you have time learning on the job in your chosen industry and get paid for this), or joint degrees that combine your original subject choice with a second subject.
- **Financial.** What are the costs? What bursaries/other funds are available? What's the graduate employment rate afterwards?
- **Other factors.** What's the accommodation like, for example? What do current students think of the course, the department, the town, and so on?

Research using some of the different university guidebooks and websites. Look at both the ones that concentrate upon academic profiles (rankings, subject tables, teaching standards, research ratings etc.), and the ones that have an 'alternative' view (social scene, popularity and rates of applications).

It's also ideal if you can look through the latest copy of *Degree Course Offers* by Brian Heap (Trotman). Each university's entry requirements are listed subject by subject, and it will also show you what course variations are available.

You can also look back through Chapters 1 and 3 of this book for a range of ideas and resources to help you decide on the best course and location for you.

FINDING VACANCIES AND ADVICE

There are many places to get course information and support during the Clearing period. By far the easiest way to see all the vacancies in one place is by using the internet, and there is plenty of advice and support available to go with it. Wherever possible, make sure you have internet access during the first day of Clearing.

1 **Internet resources**

- The official list of vacancies is published on the UCAS website (www.ucas.com), so it's a great place to start. The list goes online at one minute past midnight on the day that the A level results are published. Look through for entry requirements and make an exact note of course titles and contact details. There is also plenty of straightforward advice in their Clearing section: www.ucas.com.
- Some universities and colleges also place their vacancies on their websites. Most will at least include the phone number for their Clearing hotline.
- www.scottishclearing.org is the official Clearing site for every Scottish university and college. It also links to www.s1learning.com, the Scottish course directory, to give you a wide range of ideas and contacts.

2 **Newspapers**

Many newspapers print supplements containing available courses and contact details for Clearing from the day the results come out until the process closes. These are often also reproduced on their websites. In addition, many have up-to-date and helpful articles and advice.

- The *Independent* and the *Independent on Sunday* (www.independent.co.uk), contain the official listings of all vacancies.
- The *Guardian's* Education website has vacancies that are updated directly by the universities themselves at http://education.guardian.co.uk, plus online advice from Clearing 'Agony Aunts'.

■ The *Daily Telegraph* (www.telegraph.co.uk), *The Times* and *The Sunday Times* (www.timesonline.co.uk), contain general clearing advice.

3 Helplines

■ The UCAS Clearing phone lines have extended hours available on results day and the following two days. Applicants can call UCAS on 0871 468 0468 to discuss their application or get advice on Clearing.

■ For more specific advice, the national Exam Results Hotline has trained careers advisers to help talk through all the options available by calling 0808 100 8000 (calls are free from a landline). The advisers have access to an online database, developed by the government and UCAS in conjunction with BBC Radio, which gives up-to-the-minute information about course availability.

■ Connexions personal advisers and Careers Advisers are on hand to deal with queries, offering free, impartial and confidential advice to school and college leavers on their post-exam options, particularly those in Clearing.

■ Admissions staff at universities and colleges can offer you advice on suitable courses and entry requirements. These email addresses and phone numbers are available on their Clearing pages on the UCAS website.

■ If you live in England, you can call Connexions Direct on 080 800 13 2 19 and talk to a trained adviser in confidence about stress or anything related to courses and Clearing.

CONTACTING UNIVERSITIES

Use the resources mentioned above to look for available spaces, and find out what the entry requirements are to see whether you meet them. Make a shortlist of the degrees that interest you the most, and create a list of questions to ask – such as course costs and accommodation.

As soon as you've created a shortlist, start phoning up your chosen universities or colleges to get more information and narrow your choices down further. Sit somewhere quiet where you won't be interrupted, and get yourself as organised as possible before you start. Have your UCAS number and Clearing number, A level and GCSE (or BTEC) results in front of you, plus the correct titles and codes of the courses you are interested in, your phone number, full address including postcode, and your email address. Keep a notebook and pens handy, and charge up the phone handset if necessary.

Treat the telephone process in the same way as you would approach a job interview, and try to have a professional and positive attitude no matter how stressed or upset you might feel. Don't eat, drink or smoke while you're making calls. Most importantly, take charge of the whole process yourself and make all your own decisions – don't let your mum, dad or friend call up on your behalf as nobody else knows your thoughts and preferences as well as you do.

So pick up the phone . . . and be prepared to be patient. Remember that the lines are likely to be jammed with hundreds of students potentially ringing the same place during the same hour. Keep trying and you will eventually get through to the staff at the university's Clearing hotline. They will then ask you some questions to see whether you qualify for admission, and may also pass you on to an admissions tutor. You can sometimes get a quicker response if you email admissions staff directly.

If things go well, admissions staff may make you a provisional offer either verbally or by email. They will also give you a deadline for you to decide whether you really want the place. As you can contact as many universities and colleges as you like, you may receive informal offers from several of these.

‘ Universities get the A level results before they are released to students, so we can see who has made or missed their conditional offers and update our systems accordingly. When we go to Clearing we have about five-to-eight applicants for every available place. We are polite but firm so we can get through them as quickly as possible. We always check whereabouts the caller is, and if they have someone they can talk to when they get off the phone – whether that's a family member or someone from their school or college. Don't be scared of us! We're nice. Most of all, act like an adult and we will treat you like one. You can cry with terror before and after you have called us, but while we are speaking on the phone try and keep a handle on things. 🥯

When students have missed their offer and lost their place I would say almost all of them are anxious and 20% will be crying. All of them are very quiet – most of them know at the back of their minds there isn't much chance of getting in. In my first year of doing this job I foolishly said to one girl that she was 18 and she had the rest of her life ahead of her – she replied that her life was over and hung up. I have felt terrible about that ever since. 🥯

Most students applying to our school generally know our offers are ABB at A level – including biology and chemistry. You do get people who ring without these grades to try their luck but grades are the first thing we check so the call ends fairly quickly. For our school, the only thing that will get you in is making the grade. If you don't make our requirements, that's it. It doesn't matter how nice you are, how sweet you are, how angry or sad you are. If you don't make the requirements for the course, the person on the phone will tell you straight away and advise you accordingly. (We would normally suggest trying a different institution, or taking a year to retake whatever is letting you down and re-apply. There is no sort of penalty for re-applying in the following session). 🥯

Personally I hate it when students don't call up for themselves, and let parents or friends make the call. I had one parent who actually said, "But it's our dream to come to King's", rather than "my son's dream", which really rubbed me up the wrong way. Luckily they said it to me and not an admissions tutor, and while I don't think this was make-or-break, it would depend on the person making the decision. We only want to accept people who really want to come to our uni and who'll be happy here – not people who are trying to please their parents, or (even worse) have been forced into a decision by their parents (it happens). This is because happier students get better grades and they're less likely to drop out halfway through. Our policy is we will not discuss your personal info with anyone other than yourself. We generally ask the parent/friend to get you to call in yourself. It's much better if you ring yourself because you will be able to answer any questions much more quickly than someone else ringing in for you. '

You must have your UCAS application number and your Clearing number. We're not being pedantic. We cannot find your particular record without it and if your name is, for example, James Wilson or Seema Begum, there's a huge chance you will not be the only one and we really can't afford to take the risk of mixing up two records – I don't think this has ever happened, but it is easy to see how it could. '

If you have relevant work experience, then tell us. Admissions tutors will look favourably on anything that demonstrates you are genuinely interested in the course. For example, I know that dentistry tutors look kindly on people who can demonstrate a high

level of motor dexterity – such as model making,
etc. – as this will come in useful during the course. ﹐

If you hold an offer with another uni and you've
decided to decline it, let them know straight away so
you can be released. If you are still down as 'belonging'
to another institution, you can't be considered for
Clearing. Don't try to fudge it or lie, we can see on
the UCAS site if you haven't been released! ﹐

If you do make the requirements we will take your
details and pass them on to an admissions tutor to
make a final decision. The people answering the phones
within our school cannot make a decision. We can't even
guess what the outcome might be as we don't know how
many people our colleagues might have passed through
to be considered. You won't be able to talk to one of our
admissions tutors on the phone straight away. They are
too busy getting hold of UCAS forms and discussing who
to take etc. However, it will probably be an admissions
tutor who calls you back should you be successful. ﹐

Ask during your initial phone call for an idea of how
long it'll take for someone to call you, and then call
in if you haven't heard the day after that. Our Clearing
decisions are generally made within 24 hours, so make
sure it's easy for people to get hold of you so you can
accept or decline the place. If they call you back with an
offer (and you want to accept), you'll need to add the
course to UCAS Track as quickly as possible. Until your

application is received we can't accept you, even if the UCAS website is showing that you've been released. **⟩**

IMOGEN SALTER IS A STUDENT ADMINISTRATOR AT KING'S COLLEGE LONDON WHO WORKS ON THEIR CLEARING HOTLINE IN AUGUST.

MAKING YOUR DECISION

Shop around carefully and don't jump at the first offer you get unless you're sure it's exactly the course you really want. Go back through all your preferences and requirements one more time to make certain it's a good match. Once institutions have made you provisional/informal offers, you can only apply for one Clearing place at a time. Be certain you're fully interested and committed to this place, as higher education is a huge investment of time and money. If you need a second opinion, talk to teachers or careers advisers at your school or college, call one of the helplines mentioned on page 158, and chat with friends and relatives – but remember that only you can make the final decision. If you need to, call back or email to ask the admissions tutor any remaining questions you might still have.

Darren Barker from UCAS advises students holding provisional offers that: 'The most important thing to consider is whether they are 100% sure that this is the course for them, as they will probably be spending at least three years on the course. Before they accept, they should do some preparation and research into the course and institution to make sure that this is the right one for them.'

☑ TIP

DON'T use UCAS Track to apply for Clearing courses without first discussing vacancies with the universities themselves. You must wait for institutions to make you an informal offer first. If you do accidentally jump the gun, this may delay the progress of any application.

ACCEPTING A PLACE

Once you're certain that the place you've been offered is the right option for you, log in to UCAS Track and officially apply for your favourite Clearing place.

The admissions tutor then formally accepts you onto the course by contacting UCAS themselves. UCAS will then update your Choices page on Track to confirm that you have been officially accepted. UCAS then contact you by letter to confirm your place and provide further information.

By taking up this place, you are accepting the college or university's terms and conditions. It is a serious contractual agreement. If you change your mind about start dates or entry point, you must contact the university to discuss this – you may not necessarily be able to change them. Also, if you accept a Clearing place and then wish to cancel it, be aware that technically you cannot apply to another university or college for the same year.

> ❝ I originally planned to go to Nottingham University to study Philosophy with American Studies. When I got my A level results I had missed the grades I needed to get into Nottingham. I was devastated on results day: I remember phoning my parents in floods of tears – I was lucky that they dropped everything to come and help me or else I would have been a right mess! I remember being picked up from the school and taken home, then one of them went to buy the newspaper with all the clearing listings and then I got to looking where I wanted to go and we did some research on the internet. If it wasn't for the support of my family I think the stress would have gotten the better of me and I would have spent the next few days sulking rather than sorting out my new university place. ❞

> ❝ I was accepted into my second choice of university – Lancaster. But I had already (pre results day) decided that wasn't where I wanted to go if it came down to it. This did complicate the Clearing process a little as it meant I had to contact Lancaster to be "released" before I could apply through the Clearing system. ❞

❝ I chose based on the subject I wanted to do – which really narrowed it down as American Studies wasn't offered that widely. At one point I remember being torn between King's College London and Leicester (I could see the look of panic on my mum's face at the thought of me moving to London at that point). I ended up deciding against it as the extra cost was too much and it felt a little too close to home to give me the proper university experience I was looking for. I don't remember having any interviews, although I did talk to members of the department over the phone a few times over the days post-results. I remember basically deciding on Leicester University straight away and arranging to go to an open day a couple of days later; there wasn't much deliberation as I had my heart set on going to university that year – I think I just decided to go for it. **❞**

❝ I remember talking to Professor Martin Halliwell at the open day. He was fantastic, so friendly and welcoming and really helpful when it came to the complications of me being released from Lancaster – he was willing to hold my place on the course for me despite the delays. I mainly spoke directly to the American Studies department to get everything arranged and I can't fault them: they were so helpful and patient. **❞**

❝ I don't remember being given any advice, other than to be patient – which is actually very good advice. It isn't a straightforward process, so you do need to be patient. My main advice is to be open-minded. Before I opened my results I just assumed that all was going to be okay and I would go to the university I had planned to, and enjoy all that university had to offer. Whilst at the time it felt like my whole world had fallen apart, by being open-minded I still went on to go to a great university, to study the course I wanted and to enjoy uni life. I did have to compromise on the en-suite single room I had hoped for. . . but even that wasn't that big a deal. **"**

My other advice for anyone going through clearing:

- **Don't give up:** if you want to go to uni then go for it. There's a course out there for you!
- **Be patient:** if the phone is engaged, keep trying. Someone will answer eventually, but don't expect it to be all sorted in a day.
- **Be open-minded:** it might not be the uni you chose at first, but as long as it ticks some boxes then don't rule it out (does it do the course you are looking for?; roughly how near/far from home do you want to be?; is it a city or a campus uni?) Don't narrow it down too much, too soon.
- **Be rational:** or if you can't be, then make sure you have someone around you who can. I started looking at linguistics courses at one point 'because it looked cool', but luckily my parents were there to point out that up until that point I had no interest in linguistics and it would be a bit silly/impulsive to sign away three years of my life in a fit of panic about needing to find a place. **"**

I loved my Clearing course and the uni was fantastic. As soon as you're accepted, no-one remembers that you came through Clearing – so you just get on with it and have fun. Since uni I have been working in PR, and have recently moved to a job working in Social Media. I think my degree has been a huge help in my career – the year abroad gave me something a little bit different and by finding a course that I loved, it helped me realise the sort of thing I enjoy doing. I loved the variety of studying different subjects around a theme and this is something I look for now in my day job. I wouldn't change going through Clearing – I'm sure for whatever reason that Leicester University was the place for me and whatever route I took to get there, I'm still glad I did. **,**

JEN RILEY GRADUATED TWO YEARS AGO WITH A BA IN AMERICAN STUDIES FROM LEICESTER UNIVERSITY, WHICH INCLUDED A YEAR ABROAD.

WHAT ARE THE OTHER OPTIONS?

After starting Clearing, you may find that your grades aren't high enough to get you onto any of the courses you want, the spaces may have already been snapped up if you weren't quick enough off the mark, or you may simply decide that none of the available places interest you. If that's the case, you still have a variety of options.

- Many students take re-sits to improve their A level grades in one or more of their courses, and if this goes well they then reapply to universities the following year. If that sounds appealing, start by speaking to your school or college tutors to discuss the suitability of re-sits. Be honest about why you didn't get such good results in the first place: were you too tired or stressed, unwell, under-prepared, or struggling with the content of the A levels? You will need to act quickly if you decide on this option, and go through the same exam centre and exam board.

- You might decide to go straight into the world of employment, either with or without an element of vocational training. Talk to the careers adviser at your school or college, or contact the nearest local careers advisory service. Contact a trained adviser at www.connexions-direct. com, or look at the Directgov website for advice about choosing a career and finding and applying for jobs (www.direct.gov.uk). You could also consider an apprenticeship (www.apprenticeships.org. uk), or go to night school to get more qualifications.

- Some students undertake a mixture of re-sits, paid work and/or a gap year abroad or in the UK. To find out more about gap years, start by looking at www.gapyear.com, and asking questions in their online forums – don't just take off without any preparation.

- Some universities are now offering one-year foundation courses in a variety of subjects, and these prepare students to enter a relevant degree course when they finish. You can ask Clearing helpline advisers about these courses, to see whether their institution runs them and has any spaces left.
- You may wish to study for a degree a little later in life after you have more work experience. Examples of this include part-time degrees with evening lectures, distance learning, and the Open University (see Chapter 3 for more information).
- Some helpful advice websites and hotlines are listed on pages 158 and 180 in this book, to get you started.

WHAT IS THE ADJUSTMENT PROCESS?

Adjustment is a relatively new UCAS service, allowing you to apply for additional courses if you find you've done better than expected in your exams. It is available only to students who have **met AND exceeded** the conditions of their firm choice (FC).

Darren Barker from UCAS says that:

....

❛ The Adjustment process began in the 2009 cycle. Previous to this, applicants had been known to contact alternative universities when they found they had received higher grades than they were expecting. UCAS decided that it would be beneficial for both the applicant and the institution to provide an official way to do this. Adjustment isn't really an improvement on the Clearing system; it's a completely separate service. ❜

Adjustment opens for registration on the day that A level results are published (the 18th of August in 2011), and ends on the last day of August. There is a very short window of opportunity, so be aware of the time constraints if you think you might wish to use the service.

☑ **TIP**

If you qualify to use Adjustment, note that you only have five days to find a new place from the moment you become eligible. Check your UCAS Track page regularly to see exactly when you can start, and be prepared to act quickly.

WHO IS ELIGIBLE TO USE THE ADJUSTMENT PROCESS?

The criteria for being able to use the Adjustment process are relatively strict. You can apply for Adjustment places via UCAS only if you meet the following conditions:

- you hold a conditional firm choice (CF), and have met and exceeded the conditions that that institution gave to you, AND
- you have paid the full UCAS application fee. If you have paid a single UCAS application fee then you need to pay an extra fee to use Adjustment – this will be a £10 payment in 2011.

You can NOT use Adjustment if:

- your original offer was unconditional, OR
- you have a confirmed place on a changed course offer, OR
- you have met the conditions of your CF offer but not exceeded them.

'Meeting and exceeding your offer' is very specific to each individual student. You need to look at exactly what the college or university asked you for in the first place. For example, if you are asked to gain BBB grades at A level, and you gain ABB grades, you have both met and exceeded your offer and can use Adjustment if you wish. However, if you are asked specifically to gain BBB grades and you then take an extra A level and gain BBBB grades, you have met the exact offer but not exceeded it – the institution only asked you for three A levels, and that is all it will take into account.

It becomes slightly more complicated when students are asked to gain specific grades in certain subjects. For example, you might be asked to gain CCD grades at A level including a C grade in Chemistry. If you gain ACD with A in Chemistry then you can use Adjustment, but if you gain ACD with D in Chemistry then you can't use Adjustment (you might still wish to rethink your choice of course or university though – see page 167 for other possible options).

THINGS TO CONSIDER BEFORE TRYING ADJUSTMENT

Adjustment can potentially offer you some exciting new opportunities, but there are also several practicalities to consider and you need to have realistic expectations.

- **It's optional.** The Adjustment process is not something that appeals to everyone who is eligible to use it. If you're not sure, talk it though with an adviser.
- **Your older research can help.** Look back at your original research from when you were first searching for higher education places. You might find there was a course that you really liked, but didn't apply for or get a place on, and decide to try for that with your new A level grades. Or you may become convinced that your original firm choice (FC) is still the one for you.
- **Places are few.** It is rare for the most competitive courses to have places available, and there's no guarantee that you'll find what you're looking for. In the last academic year, 382 students secured places through Adjustment, compared with the 47,673 students who were accepted through Clearing.
- **Vacancies change every day.** Students already accepted onto courses drop out for a variety of reasons on a daily basis, and these numbers are updated quickly by the respective universities and colleges. If a course you like doesn't have a space on it today, you might still be lucky if you call up tomorrow, or the day after.
- **Safety net.** On the plus side, if you try to find a different course through Adjustment then you won't risk losing out on the university place you've already gained. Your original firm choice (FC) becomes an unconditional firm choice (UF) and is kept safe for you while you're looking and applying, and if you can't find a suitable new place then you can still stick to your original plan if you want.
- **Practicalities.** If you find a new course through Adjustment, remember that you could end up arranging finance and accommodation at the last minute. You may also need to cancel previous arrangements at your original firm choice.

▶ **Changing your mind.** However, if you rush into accepting a new Adjustment place, there could be trouble ahead if you then decide to change your mind. Once you've been accepted for a new place, your original unconditional firm choice (UF) is informed and the UF place will no longer be held for you. If you want to go back to your original UF choice, you will first have to get your Adjustment choice to agree to withdraw your offer and release you, and you will then have to enter Clearing to see whether your original UF choice can still offer you a place.

HOW THE ADJUSTMENT PROCESS WORKS

1 A level results are published

2 Check you qualify for Adjustment

3 Your conditional firm choice (FC) changes to unconditional firm choice (UF) on UCAS Track

4 Register online to use Adjustment (click the link that appears on your Choices screen in Track)

5 Research new degree courses

6 Contact universities and colleges

7 Institution(s) may offer you a place

8 You accept the new place

9 New course replaces your original unconditional firm choice (UF) on UCAS Track

10 UCAS send you a confirmation letter

FINDING ADJUSTMENT PLACES

There is currently no central database where you can look at all available Adjustment vacancies, so you need to look in several different places to find them.

Darren Barker from UCAS advises that: 'People can use the Clearing vacancy search to look for courses that may require higher entry requirements that the applicant now has, but mostly an applicant will contact a university directly about a course they otherwise wouldn't have been able to get on. The process is then formalised through UCAS.' He also says that, 'Some universities will advertise on their website that they have places available through Adjustment.'

COURSE FINDING CHECKLIST

- Remind yourself about ways to search for new courses by re-reading pages 3–31 of this book.
- Go back through any notes you made about different courses when you started your original application. Be specific about what you really want.
- Phone up institutions you like the look of, and ask about places. Ask specifically about Adjustment opportunities.
- If you can't get through on the phone, send an email instead.
- Be prepared to follow up phone calls and emails if you aren't answered, and be proactive.
- Look at different university and college websites – some of them advertise Adjustment places, but not all.
- Look at newspapers and websites, including the UCAS site, for a quick idea of Clearing vacancies that might be a good fit for your new grades. These places could also be available via Adjustment.

☑ TIP

Keep good notes about which universities/colleges you call, including times and dates, what was said, and the name of the person you spoke to. You may need to refer back to these notes while you're making important decisions.

HOW TO APPLY FOR ADJUSTMENT PLACES

After you have registered online with UCAS to use Adjustment, done your course research and contacted universities and colleges about Adjustment vacancies, one or more of these institutions may want to consider you. If this happens, they will ask you for your UCAS personal ID, so have your details to hand. They will then view your application and probably also wish to hold a telephone interview with you.

If they make you an offer, this is usually done over the phone and then followed up with a confirmation email to you. If you decide to accept an offer, you send them a confirmation email in return, and the institution notifies UCAS that you have accepted the place. Once this is done, your UCAS Track page will update with your new course details. At the same time, your original firm choice is given up and made available to someone else. Once this is confirmed you will probably need to make new student finance and accommodation arrangements too.

YOUR OPTIONS IF ADJUSTMENT DOESN'T WORK OUT

Not everyone is lucky enough to find a place through Adjustment. Last year from a total of 3,600 registrations, 384 were placed in their Adjustment choice, 2,355 reconfirmed with their original choice and 444 were placed in another choice (mostly via Clearing). Also, 417 of those who registered for Adjustment were not placed (and did not go to university or college that year).

If you get better grades than you were expecting you still have lots of options. You can:

- stick with your original choice of course (it's automatically kept safe for you)
- try to persuade your chosen university/college to let you move to a different course
- give up your original firm choice and risk going through Clearing to try to find a course
- withdraw from the UCAS application process for the current year, then apply for the following year's academic intake (this gives you the full range of course options for that year, and could be especially helpful if you gained very high grades and now wish to apply for a popular course).

If you can't decide which one of these options is best for you, talking it through with a trained and unbiased adviser can be very helpful.

' I "firmed" a place in May, but I didn't really intend on going there, I just wanted a backup in case I decided against gap-yearing. On results day I'd exceeded my offer by three grades (they wanted AAB, I got A*A*A) so I figured I may as well sign up to Adjustment, but after looking around the websites of unis that interested me – Exeter, Bristol, Leeds and York – all of them said they had no places for Adjustment or Clearing. That's completely unsurprising: they're all really competitive, and I was looking for English Literature places, which is even more competitive. '

' UCAS didn't help at all in terms of finding places that were in Adjustment though. It was up to me to try and find courses, so it's nothing like Clearing where it tells you the options available. The process is easy to use in terms of the UCAS website and signing up for it, but I didn't find it successful. I'm not sure I would have taken a place even if I had found one, as I hadn't visited any of the unis I was looking at and I highly doubt they would have been able to offer me on-site accommodation. I decided I was happier gap-yearing and reapplying, so that's what I did. '

VICKY TURNBULL, AGE 18, CURRENTLY TAKING A GAP YEAR

SUMMARY:
TOP TIPS FOR CLEARING AND ADJUSTMENT SUCCESS

1. Be there. One of the commonest complaints from universities and colleges during Clearing time is that many students are away on holiday when their A level results are published. If something goes wrong you need to be there in person to sort it out, so don't plan your vacation for the middle of August, especially if you're going overseas. The same is also true for the very brief Adjustment period.

2. Don't panic. You need to think clearly and calmly, and be rational. Making a sudden panicky decision about a course or a location could negatively affect your life for many years to come, and it increases your chances of dropping out of university.

3. Act quickly. While it's important not to panic, it's also important not to be frozen by fear or be too laid back. You need to get moving. In recent years, the most sought-after places have been snapped up increasingly quickly, with whole courses often being filled during the first 24 to 48 hours.

4. Do lots of research. Find out about alternative institutions and courses via helplines, newspapers, websites and careers advisers. Remember some courses that initially sound very different can be extremely similar in their content and structure, so keep looking.

5. Be flexible if in Clearing. During Clearing you can apply for courses that are completely different from the ones you originally applied for. Have a rough idea to help you narrow down your search, but at the same time keep an open mind. Don't automatically discount suggestions.

6. Be organised. When researching courses, make a shortlist. Then gather together all your important information in one place (including Clearing number or UCAS ID, A level and GCSE grades, your phone number and email) and start by phoning the college or university at the top of your list.

7. Be polite and treat it like a job interview. You need to make a good impression and show the people at the end of the phone/email that you're keen and motivated. Mention all relevant experience and interests that could give you the edge.

8. You don't have to take the first offer. If an offer is made, take your time and don't rush into an immediate decision. Call back and ask more questions if you want to, take a virtual tour of the university or school on their website, and visit in person if you think you have time.

9. Confirm your place correctly. To accept an informal Clearing offer you must apply for the course using Track, then wait for official confirmation via UCAS. If you accept an Adjustment place you must confirm verbally, then return the university's email, and then wait for the university or college to notify UCAS.

10. Consider other options. Not everyone decides to go through Clearing or Adjustment, or finds a place through these processes. Your other possible choices could include a gap year, and/or reapplying next year. Other students may decide to take a foundation course, re-sit exams to improve their grades, undertake vocational training, apply for a job or even start their own business.

FURTHER READING

BOOKS
Background research before you apply
- *Choosing Your Degree Course and University*, Brian Heap (Trotman Publishing)
- *Heap 2012: University Degree Course Offers*, Brian Heap (Trotman Publishing)
- *The Guardian University Guide*, Kristen Harrison and Chris Addison (Guardian Books)
- *The Times Good University Guide*, John O'Leary (Times Books)
- *The Virgin Guide to British Universities*, Piers Dudgeon (Virgin Books)

Funding & finance
- *University Scholarships, Awards and Bursaries*, Brian Heap (Trotman Publishing)
- *The Guide to Student Money 2011*, Gwenda Thomas (Trotman Publishing)
- *The Complete University Guide: Student Finance*, Bernard Kingston and Nicola Chalton (Right Way)

Gap year
- *Your Gap Year*, Susan Griffith (Vacation Work)
- *The Gap Year Guidebook*, Alison Withers (John Catt Ltd)

Interview skills
- *Young Jobhunters: Interview Skills*, Helen Cooper (Trotman Publishing)
- *You're Hired! Interview*, Judi James (Trotman Publishing)
- *Perfect Interview*, Max Eggert (Random House)

Open days

🚩 *Open Days* (UCAS)

WEBSITES
Admissions tests

🚩 www.admissionstests.cambridgeassessment.org.uk/adt/bmat

🚩 www.admissionstests.cambridgeassessment.org.uk/adt/elat

🚩 www.gamsatuk.org

🚩 www.hpat.org.uk

🚩 www.history.ox.ac.uk/prosundergrad/applying/hat_introduction.htm

🚩 www.ox.ac.uk/admissions/undergraduate_courses/how_to_apply/tests/index.html

🚩 www.cam.ac.uk/admissions/undergraduate/courses/mml/tests.html

🚩 www.ox.ac.uk/admissions/undergraduate_courses/how_to_apply/tests/index.html

🚩 www.admissionstests.cambridgeassessment.org.uk/adt/step

🚩 http://www.admissionstests.cambridgeassessment.org.uk/adt/tsacambridge

🚩 www.admissionstests.cambridgeassessment.org.uk/adt/tsaoxford

🚩 www.admissionstests.cambridgeassessment.org.uk/adt/tsaucl

🚩 www.ukcat.ac.uk

Background research before you apply

🚩 www.centigradeonline.co.uk

🚩 www.coursediscoveronline.co.uk

🚩 www.cukas.ac.uk

🚩 www.dcfs.gov.uk/recognisedukdegrees

🚩 www.direct.gov.uk

🚩 www.educationuk.org (the British Council)

🚩 www.fasttomato.com

🚩 www.guardian.co.uk/education/series/university-guide-2011-subjects

🚩 www.hesa.ac.uk

🚩 www.learndirect.co.uk

🚩 www.qaa.ac.uk

🚩 www.thestudentroom.co.uk

🚩 www.ucas.com

🚩 www.unistats.com

- www.whatuni.com
- www.yougo.co.uk

Clearing

- www.ucas.com
- www.scottishclearing.org
- www.independent.co.uk/student
- http://education.guardian.co.uk
- www.telegraph.co.uk
- www.timesonline.co.uk

Funding

- www.scholarship-search.org.uk
- www.direct.gov.uk/en/EducationAndLearning/ UniversityAndHigherEducation/StudentFinance/ www.hero.ac.uk/uk/ studying/funding_your_study263.cfm

Gap year

- www.gapadvice.org
- www.gapyear.com
- www.yearoutgroup.org/calendar.htm

Information for students with special needs

- www.skill.org.uk

League tables

- www.timesonline.co.uk
- http://extras.timesonline.co.uk/stug/universityguide.php
- www.guardian.co.uk/education/universityguide
- www.thecompleteuniversityguide.co.uk

Open days

- www.ucas.com/events
- www.opendays.com/calendar

Study abroad

- www.cao.ie/index.php
- www.braintrack.com
- www.ukcisa.org.uk/student/ukstudent/index.php

Teacher training

- www.tda.gov.uk
- www.gttr.ac.uk

Work and careers

- www.direct.gov.uk/en/YoungPeople/Workandcareers/index.htm
- www.connexions-direct.com
- www.apprenticeships.org.uk
- www.connexions-direct.com/jobs4u
- www.prospects.ac.uk/jobs_and_work_experience.htm
- www.prospects.ac.uk/options_with_your_subject.htm
- www.agr.org.uk
- www.highfliers.co.uk
- https://nextstep.direct.gov.uk/planningyourcareer/jobprofiles/Pages/default.aspx